The Ancient Pathways of Heaven

A Journey into the Unseen Realm

by

Jeremy Friedman

The Ancient Pathways of Heaven

A Journey into the Unseen Realm

by

Jeremy Friedman

Lighthouse Family Ministries, Inc.
8250 Silver Birch Way
Lehigh Acres, Florida 33971
USA
www.LighthouseFM.net

The Ancient Pathways of Heaven
A Journey into the Unseen Realm

Copyright © 2023 Jeremy Friedman

Scripture is taken from the New King James Version®. Copyright © 1982 by Thomas Nelson. Used by permission. All rights reserved. (Unless otherwise noted.)

Scripture quotations marked (ESV) are from the ESV® EBible (The Holy Bible, English Standard Version®), copyright © 2001 by Crossway, a publishing ministry of Good News Publishers. Used by permission. All rights reserved.

Scripture quotations marked (AMP) are taken from the Amplified® Bible, Copyright © 1954, 1958, 1962, 1964, 1965, 1987 by The Lockman Foundation.

Scripture quotations marked (TLV) are taken from the Tree of Life Version of the Bible. Copyright © 2023 Messianic Jewish Family Bible Society | DBA: Tree of Life Bible Society. All rights reserved.

Scripture quotations are taken from the Holy Bible, New Living Translation (NLT), copyright © 1996, 2004, 2007, 2013, 2015 by Tyndale House Foundation. Used by permission of Tyndale House Publishers, Inc., Carol Stream, Illinois 60188. All rights reserved.

Scripture marked (TPT) is taken from the The Passion Translation Copyright © 2017, 2018 by Passion & Fire Ministries, Inc. Used by permission. All rights reserved. ThePassionTranslation.com

All rights reserved. This book is protected by the copyright laws of the United States of America. This book may not be copied or reprinted for commercial gain or profit. The use of short quotations or occasional page copying for personal, or group study is permitted and encouraged. Permission will be granted upon request.

Requests for bulk sales discounts, editorial permissions, or other information should be addressed to:

Scroll Publishers
PO Box 5847
Pinehurst, NC 28374 USA

Additional copies available at www.ScrollPublishers.com

ISBN 13 TP: 978-1-962808-00-2
ISBN 13 eBook: 978-1-962808-01-9

Cover Design by Darian Horner Design
(www.darianhorner.com)
Image: stock.adobe.com #415903913

First Edition: November 2023

10 9 8 7 6 5 4 3 2 1

Printed in the United States of America

Table of Contents

Acknowledgements i

Foreword iii

Preface v

Chapter 1 Ancient Doors & Paths 1

Chapter 2 Possessing Gates 11

Chapter 3 Foundations of the Blueprints of Destiny 19

Chapter 4 Revelation of Destiny Scrolls 21

Chapter 5 Perfectly Laid Plans 29

Chapter 6 Stars, Destinies, and Trade Routes 33

Chapter 7 Intertwining of Blueprints, Destiny Scrolls,
Star Maps, and Trade Routes 37

Chapter 8 The Tunnel of Time 45

Chapter 9 Time Angels & Time Gates 49

Chapter 10 The Frequencies of Heavenly Healing 61

Chapter 11 Restoration & Awestruck Wonder 67

Chapter 12 Father's Garden 73

Chapter 13 Joy & Jubilee of the Lord 81

Chapter 14 Place of the Miraculous 87

Chapter 15 River of Grace 91

Chapter 16 Encounter with the Spirit of Faith 103

Chapter 17 Encounter with the Citizens of Heaven 111

Chapter 18 Encounter with the Goodness of God 121

Chapter 19 The Armies of Heaven 127

Chapter 20 Exposing and Defeating Darkness 133

Chapter 21 Pressing Through Opposition 145

Characters in this Book 157

Description 161

About the Author 163

Acknowledgements

This book is dedicated first and foremost to God, for without His divine intervention, the power of His love, and the mighty works of His miracle healing power, I would not be here to share the information. I wish to thank my beautiful and devoted wife, Joelene, a true Proverbs 31 woman, for her support and contributions to the editing process.

Lastly, I wish to acknowledge and honor my dear friend, mentor, and spiritual father, Dr. Ron M. Horner. With his encouragement, teaching, and apostolic leadership, I have been provoked to seek the deeper things of the Kingdom of Heaven. I hope this book will stir a hunger and thirst deep within you to seek deeper intimacy with Our Heavenly Father and all the glorious riches He has for you.

Foreword

A little over four years ago, while conducting a mentoring class, Jeremy Friedman came into my life. He was an ardent student of the Courts of Heaven, which I was teaching at that time. He and the handful of others who had joined us for that mentoring class were to embark on discoveries far beyond their imagination at the time.

As time passed, Jeremy and several of the others in the class continued to connect with our ministry (LifeSpring International Ministries). Jeremy was a student in our Facilitator's Training Program and became involved as a Junior Advocate, helping people navigate the Courts of Heaven. Eventually, he became the head of our Heaven Down Business™ entity, which coaches entrepreneurs and business people in building their businesses from the Heaven Down paradigm.

I have been honored to watch Jeremy grow in his faith and in fatherhood. I also have watched as he lives at home what he preaches in the public square. With his beautiful wife Joelene, they are raising Kingdom equippers in their children.

I want to congratulate Jeremy on this, the first of many books that share his experiences in the realms of Heaven and that encourage others to have their own encounters. The ancient paths that Jeremy has walked are available to you as well. Enjoy!

Dr. Ron M. Horner
Author

Preface

The Bible, the infallible Word of God, given to man by the inspiration of the Holy Spirit, is a book of power, depth, spiritual truth, and a blueprint for life. Much of what is written in the canonical texts are collections of journals written by our fathers in the faith. These journals have been passed down from generation to generation as a testament to what God has done, has promised to do, and will continue to do until His Kingdom has fully come. We have a track record that He is always good, faithful, and ever present.

To this day, the Bible's divine contents are still not fully understood. Many ancient paths of biblical wisdom have long been forgotten. Revelation has been lost or destroyed through the ages and, in some cases, controlled by the powers of spiritual wickedness in operation on the earth. The book you hold is a collection of such journals and revelations that have been given over time simply by seeking the Kingdom of Heaven, inclining an ear to listen, and being obedient to record all that is spoken. As we enter the revelatory age, the Lord is restoring what has been lost to His children.

All the children of God, who have given their hearts to the Lord and embraced the precious gift of the Holy Spirit, have been given this access. We, as sons, can come to the Father, sit at His table, and feast with him. As you read this book, I pray you receive deliverance, breakthrough, healing, and an insatiable hunger to hear Heaven for yourself. May you be blessed with new hope, courage, and boldness. Allow Holy Spirit to flow through you so that others may glean from the treasures He pours out. It is by freely giving that we freely receive.

Chapter 1
Ancient Doors & Paths

On the morning of December 21st, 2022, during my prayer time, I stepped into Heaven and saw rivers of water that were flowing into large doorways. The Holy Spirit revealed to me that these were the ancient doors that led to the ancient paths. I was instantly transported back to a dream I had many years earlier. In the dream, the Father was running a meeting in a giant conference room of an office building. The Father was the CEO, sending me and many others out into the field to labor and collect a harvest. As I pondered the dream and its meaning, the Holy Spirit said, "The ancient doors are portals."

I asked Heaven for some tutoring assistance and clarification to better understand the meaning of this. Instantly, a man in white stood before me; his name was Mitchell. As Mitchell came forth, I noticed he had company; Jeremiah, the prophet, was with him. I asked if they could impart to me some expanded revelation on the purpose of the ancient doors and paths. I had also requested they provide an understanding of how they work.

Mitchell began to teach me by saying, "The ancient doors are structures that seed is poured out of, and harvest is collected through. They are portals as well as gates; they are as old as creation, as real and important in function as the windows of Heaven."

Mitchell said, "When you read in the book of Genesis about Jacob's dream of the ladder, it's the ladder that led to an ancient door. The ancient doors are passageways between points of time and space, between Heaven and Earth. They are the gates to the pathways and highways that traverse Heaven to carry what is released into being. These doors are vehicles for the prayers of the saints to be collected through, as well as narrow ways for the saints to travel in the spirit to reach the Father's realms. They are the places in eternity He has set within their hearts."

Jeremiah began, "These are merely the places of righteousness. The places that have been apportioned for the sons of God to travel to and through. When accessing these ancient paths, righteousness must be your intent; otherwise, these gates will shut themselves up.

Referencing the Word of God, Jeremiah pointed out:

Because My people have forgotten Me, they have burned incense to worthless idols. And they have caused themselves to stumble in their ways, from the ancient paths, to walk in pathways and not on a highway. (Jeremiah 18:15) (NKJV)

The pathways are those of peace and seeking out the Father's hidden heavenly riches for His sons. Those who do not know the Father cannot access these hidden riches in Heavenly places. The ones who have His Spirit within them and have been adopted within the family of God are themselves keys. They are keys that vibrate at the resonant frequencies of Jesus and God the Father. This is the frequency of the blood and that which activates these doors and paths to be in operation for a time."

They noticed I looked confused, so Mitchell said, "Think of it as a car on a roadway that comes to a dead end. That dead end is the path the world travels. However, for the saints, that dead end doesn't exist. It is a tunnel that leads to more roads, and He makes a way where there is no way."

"Faith opens these paths, and they are the portals through which prayers are answered and released. Angels come through these doors to provide Heavenly healing, help, sustenance, and more. The list is endless. These incorruptible gates can only be possessed by those of the Father's Kingdom. They cannot be captured, encroached upon, or stolen. They are used by God for His Kingdom and those of His family for good." After this was spoken to me, the encounter ended.

New Pathways

In another engagement, I was taken into an encounter where I could see laser lights that appeared as race cars. They looked like the vehicles from the movie *Tron*. The Holy Spirit revealed to me that they represented the lightnings of God on pathways that are opening, traversing, and connecting from your heavenly destiny to your earthly dominion. These are the callings, mandates, and assignments from Heaven brought into the earth. They are for the saints of Heaven to partake in and partner with Heaven to fulfill the calling that is key and innate to each believer.

A believer's calling is like a snowflake or a fingerprint. No two callings are alike. One may be called, commissioned, and gifted similarly to another, but each individual's call is unique in execution. The lightning's resonant frequency moves obstacles out of the believer's path. It generates a frequency known as *the Glory* that the Holy Spirit, the angels, and all beings of the Third Heaven carry. The frequency you feel when you know to share your testimony, glorify God, and pray in an uncharacteristic location can transform realms and lives and assist the sons and daughters of God in fulfilling their mandates. It is a marker and identifier of the divine appointments and steps that the Lord has ordered. Be bold in the Lord and willing to do all He has called you to do for His purposes.

Paths of Wisdom

Stepping into Heaven on another occasion, I was ushered into the Court of Wisdom. When I entered, I saw a hearth with the fireplace lit; it was warm. I stuck my hand and arm in; then, my body went ablaze with the fire of God. I was encouraged by the Holy Spirit to review my journal entries and recall the revelation I had been given to press into new realms of revelation.

Soon afterward, I saw Solomon and David; they opened a gate that allowed me access to the throne room. Upon entering, Jesus greeted me with a loving embrace, and so did the Father. They said they wanted to take me to the secret place under the shadow of His wings. As we entered the secret place, I saw the snowcapped mountains I am accustomed to seeing when I engage Heaven, but this time one was erupting like a volcano. I could see liquid hot magma dripping down from the mouth of the volcano. I asked what the significance was and was told, "This magma is the love of the Father and represents His burning desire to know every one of His children. It is the swell of emotion of the Father's heart for His beloved ones to cry out, to seek Him, and to know Him more intimately. The volcano is symbolic of His fiery love. It is the kind of love that melts all things that hinder it and creates new realities, new destinies, and new pathways for the adopted sons and daughters of God to enter into."

After being told this, a platoon of angels flew over, eleven to be exact. They had swords of fire with bluish-white flames and were massive in stature, flying in a "V" formation. The one in front handed me a scroll and a large crystal key. His name was "Hermie." He said, "This scroll and key were new entries in your destiny, as you had set your heart's intention to seek God at this particular hour and press into the access you have in a new way. A pathway had been opened for a new revelatory destiny.

As the heart grows in this intentionality of seeking the Father, the Heavenly realm expands and opens up. This is like what Yeshua spoke of in Matthew 13 about the parable of the mustard seed being like Heaven. As we grow in our intentionality of access to Heaven, the doors and expansion of corridors we can navigate open wider." "The key," he explained, "is for a Heavenly gate to 'the viewing room.' In this place, you could view various things throughout time in the natural realm and eternal realm, much like a movie." As he spoke, a golden door appeared. I inserted the key, opened the door, and saw golden light flooding in. The room looked and felt much like a movie theater.

In the spirit, through the intentionality of your heart's desire, you could view various moments. The first to be viewed was the time of my birth. I could see my parents with me at the moment I was delivered. In the Heavenly realm, I could see angels, my personal angel, Jesus, and the Father.

They were discussing, marveling over me with love, pride, and adoration. The Father then made a declaration:

Before I formed you in the womb, I knew you, and before you were born, I set you apart— I appointed you prophet to the nations. (Jeremiah 1:5) (TLV)

As he spoke this, I could see three lightnings of God, like angels, shoot down into the delivery room. One touched the baby's chest, and I saw a golden glow go inside me as an infant. "The spirit of the living God is among you," another said.

The next moment I saw, in Earth time, was a dark moment where I tried to kill myself before I was saved, but I saw the Lord simultaneously say, "Enough!" Standing up from His throne, He said, "Go to Him now, and give Him this message!" That message was entrusted to angels, the delivery of which changed the natural course of my life, saved me from death, and led me home to the Lord.

After this, I was able to see into the future. I was shown myself, my wife, our children, and our grandchildren on a mission field, loving on orphans in what looked to be on the continent of Africa or a third-world country. Standing behind us was the King of Glory, Jesus, and some of our angels. Jesus had His hands atop a royal scepter that He was leaning on, marveling over the work. I heard Him speak, "This is My son with whom I am well pleased." I could see the sheer joy in my face, watching my descendants do the Lord's work. The feeling was overwhelming and fulfilling because I now knew that the best inheritance I could leave for them was to live to serve the Lord.

A little girl ran up to me with a loaf of bread; she said, "Grandpa, Grandpa, can you pray?" As I sang the Hebrew blessing over the bread, they joined in unison. We broke it, took communion, and started singing praises to the Lord. I opened the scroll the angel had given me at that moment. It said:

> *'For I know the plans that I have in mind for you, 'declares Adonai, 'plans for shalom and not calamity, to give you a future and a hope.' (Jeremiah 29:11) (TLV)*

Door of Hope

In the early morning hours of September 9th, 2022, I had a vision as I was worshipping the Lord. He gave me three keys, and I saw a door appear with three keyholes. God, Holy Spirit, and Jesus each inserted and turned their corresponding keys, and as the door opened, I saw a beautiful valley with golden light. I heard Holy Spirit say, "Valley of Achor." I looked this up in the Word to see what the Valley of Achor was and found it mentioned in Hosea 2:15.

I will give her vineyards from there, and the Valley of Achor as a door of hope; she shall sing there, as in the days of her youth, as in the day when she came up from the land of Egypt. (Hosea 2:15) (NKJV)

This was the door of Hope.

Doorway to Destiny

Several months later, on December 30th, 2022, I stepped into Heaven and felt led to do some repentance prayer regarding spiritual seeing and removing pollution from the gates of my eyes, mind, ears, and heart. As soon as I finished praying, I noticed three men standing before me in the courtroom of Heaven. One of them was Moses; he presented me with the commandments of the Lord that they be written on my heart. Next, Abraham was there, and he handed me a rope that was being used to lead two camels. Abraham said this is an investment in the hidden riches I will begin to see in Heavenly places, the treasures of the seer dimension, and a symbol of wealth transfer. Finally, Joseph blessed me with His words and told me how uniquely I was created and how extraordinary the gift of dreams is that the Father had put inside me. As I pressed in further to see, I noticed a gate of golden light that resembled an open doorway. There, I saw a man walking through it, the skirt of his garments swaying as he walked. It was Jesus as Melchizedek, and he was dressed in the garments of the high priest. The skirt of the robes was the purest white with golden threads that had stitching and golden bells on the fringes. The chest portion was the loveliest of royal blues I had ever beheld. It was as deep and richly colored as a sparkling deep blue ocean; the chest plate had jewels upon it, many of which I had never beheld. The word 'beryl' dropped in my spirit as I gazed upon the beauty of the stones, but none of that beauty was to compare as I gazed upon the beauty of His face. Instantly, I began to weep in the natural, my body gyrating as I wept. To gaze upon the beauty of the Lord, the excitement that filled me to be adored by Him is indescribable. All I could do was cry at the purity of His love as He hugged me and spoke one word, 'Beloved.' I crumbled in the frequency of love that radiated in that word while He swung me around like a small child and grabbed my hand. He asked me if I was ready to take the next step into my destiny. As He said this, a scroll unrolled into a pathway. A staircase led to a doorway at the end of this path. I whispered, "Yes, I am ready!" He took my hand, and we walked onward. He whispered, "I will always be with you every step of the way, My beloved child!"

Chapter 2
Possessing Gates

In another revelatory encounter, I stepped into Heaven and saw my personal angel, Phillip, waiting for me. As I looked at him, I saw these pelts hanging from his belt; he said they were trophies from prior battles. Suddenly, I saw this sword of light drop down from the Heavens. It plunged into a cloud, and lightning struck the earth. As the lightning hit the earth, I saw shockwaves of frequency ripple across the surface, much like an earthquake. This lightning and the shockwaves were causing shifts in regions. I could see both the natural Earth, which seemed unmoved and unharmed, and the spiritual climates which overlaid them.

The spiritual turf was shaken up, with some areas appearing to be torn up. I heard, "These were the enemy's camps; they are losing ground and turf. These areas are being reclaimed for the Kingdom of Heaven." Suddenly, I saw the patrollers of this region appear. From a blast of the Father's' nostrils in the Heavens, I could see a torrent of wind blowing across this area. It was a wave of the Ruach of God; I saw demons and imps fleeing. I could also see thrones torn down and principalities overthrown and shaken. The armies of Heaven were in this wind.

There were many angels as well as men and women in white linen with the sons of God just behind them. They walked in sync, held hands, and walked in authority and unity. As they took each step forward, the areas of impact advanced till the shockwaves enveloped the whole Earth. I could see a small segment at the bottom of the earth that was encircled and surrounded by the massive armies of Heaven. I took notice of another massive army, the army of the bride. She was rising up in her authority, and the remnant of the enemy's camp was completely outnumbered, surrounded, and detained with nowhere to go. I heard the spirit of the Lord say, "I will put the enemy in subjection beneath your feet; rise up."

This revelation stopped, and I saw my angel pull the sword out of the cloud. He said, "This is a generational war; it goes from generation to generation until the day of the Lord has come. Train up your children in righteousness and the generations after them. Traditions of men will do them no good in this battle, but the weapons of spiritual warfare, the art of intimacy, the knowledge of the goodness of God, and the expectation of His goodness will be the keys that will lead them on the path of truth to possess the victor's crown. The spoils of this war belong to the sons of God; the territory is theirs for the taking.

Who will rise up in the day of distractions and possess His gate and the fullness of His inheritance? Who will set His face like flint to receive the fullness of what the Father intends for him?" As my angel said this, he handed me a large sword. It was bright and shiny with a blade shimmering like the whitest gold, and a handle of a burnished bronze color made of gold. I heard him say, "possess your Gate." As I rose and began to pray over this, I could hear the words "rule and reign." After this, the encounter concluded.

Gates & Dimensions

As I continued seeking more revelation, I entered into prayer one morning and instantly saw myself looking down upon a valley. A beautiful orange glow lit up the sky, almost like a sunset in the valley. I could see many houses and villages below and what appeared to be a carnival. I asked the Lord, "What is the carnival for?" He replied, "It's a celebration of the sonship of the Saints." Heaven is celebrating those walking in greater sonship these days. There is a continual celebration in the Heavens, celebrating the sons who have returned to the Father and come back home from wayward paths.

As I walked on the slope of the hill before me, I noticed Jesus was with me. There were many trees and bushes with fresh blooms of blue, purple, and white foliage.

As we continued, we came to a golden path that went through the town towards the carnival. While I was walking, I noticed many animals. One was a horse. It came up to me, and I said, "What do you have for me, horse?" Out of its mouth dropped a clear and white gemstone. It was a white sapphire, and with it was a small scroll. As I unsealed it, the scroll transformed into a golden key. I was told the key was to the door of a greater dimension of sonship, interwoven with a dominion being given over many domains, realities, and dimensions.

Suddenly, a door appeared in front of me. It was red with gold inlays and etching all over it. I twisted the key in the keyhole, and the key disappeared. The door flung open, and before me was a hallway of light. Many gates were in this hallway, on the right and the left. I was told that each gate enters a different domain, a different point in time, and, sometimes, other dimensional realities. I asked if they were carbon copies or mirror images of my world, but I was told that they were more like different dimensions or layers overlaid on top of the dimensional reality in which I live. My angel Philip said, "These are different dimensional realities, supernatural domains." He said, "When you pray prayers of in time and out of time and in every timeline, age, realm, and dimension, these gates lead to those dimensions." He also said, "These are hallways that the sons, the men in white, and Heaven's angel armies have access to in order to engage those assignments as a son of the Most High. You are called to be a gatekeeper, one who minds the gates, one who stewards and releases the stewardship of the inheritances of the sons into the earth. Release it into towns, cities, nations, and governments to effect change." After receiving this final instruction, the vision ended, leaving me with many things to ponder.

The Gate of Transformation

Entering a courtyard where Jesus stood, I bowed before Him, kissed His feet, and wept in brokenness. Holy Spirit spoke and said, "Open your mouth". As I obeyed, an angel appeared with tongs holding a piece of red-hot coal and proceeded to put it down my throat. It cleansed my realms and my heart of all darkness. Jesus then gave me three keys. The scene changed, and suddenly, we were walking down a winding staircase to a place He called the Cave of Treasures. I became aware that it was also known as the Cave of Wonders. I saw gold and jewels everywhere and a large treasure chest in the middle. Torches lit the room. I used a key to open the treasure chest, and when it unlocked, I fell into white light. Heaven said, "This light was an ocean of the light of the Lord and of His love." All I could do was weep.

During this encounter, it felt like I was completely transformed. Jesus then gave me a key to my heart. Together, we used it, and as my heart unlocked, it was opened to receive His heart and love. Many of the saints gathered around, laying hands upon me and trading His love into me. I saw white, gold, and silver clouds swirling from above, and a portal had opened in the center. The Father looked down through this portal and said, "You are My son, and with you, I am well pleased."

As I heard His voice, it shook me to my core. This encounter caused me to weep uncontrollably as I became aware of our human sin nature and felt undeserving of His love. As I wept, He said, "I did it for you." At this moment, I re-consecrated my heart and all realms to Him. Broken and crying, I said I'm just a sinner, I didn't deserve your love, but you gave your son to save me anyway, not just to save me but to use me. He said, "I love you more than anything." The Lord said, "Fire prophet, you are My fire prophet; let the fire be uproariously released from your lips."

Jesus asked me if I was ready to use the third key. I said yes, Lord! As I replied, an iron door with squiggly ornamentation appeared before me. I was told it was the "gate of dreams and transformation," the Lord opened it, reached His arm inside, and stuffed its contents inside my chest. These were His dreams and His transformational power, which resembled wet clay. I wept bitterly, feeling unworthy of His love. He molded me as a potter molds His work of art. He cut away the excess and smoothed the broken and rough edges to create the vessel of His choosing. This vessel would now contain His wonderful love, and He poured out His wondrous glory. He said, "Jeremy, you are perfect in every way." I said, "Lord, you're worthy of it all," and he replied, "My son, you are worthy of it all!!"

Star Gates

As I poised myself to press into Heaven for revelation on the morning of March 31st, 2023, I heard a discussion amongst a few voices about star gates and their use. As I asked the Holy Spirit what this was about. The reply I heard stretched my understanding. Heaven said,

> *Stargates are portals of travel throughout the cosmos, into galaxies, and connections between star systems. These portals of access have been long forgotten. Many have accessed them in the astral realm (profanely), but the sons of the Kingdom have long resisted embracing this revelation. It has been labeled as witchcraft or New Age. This is the time in which the generations will take back their identity and walk as sons, as the Father had established from the beginning of all things, well before the fall in the Garden of Eden.*

In the midst of this vision, I stopped to listen again to the voices I had heard initially. I saw that I was in the middle of a heavenly council meeting. I could sense six men there with me. Looking intently, I saw Jesus, Enoch, Job, Moses, Isaac, and Jacob seated around a table, conversing. I listened in awe as the discussion continued, completely blown away. They gave me insight and said, "Access to the astral plane is profane in nature, as many involved in occultism fraudulently access these places through witchcraft. However, in Christ, through Jesus the ONLY door, and with the mind of Christ, this is your inheritance; teleportation, transportation, bi-location, and time travel are all possible." Another added, "The Kingdom of Heaven is outside of time and space and has many portals and access points that have been long forgotten or hidden from mankind." A third said, "Let the Holy Spirit be your guide, enter in through Jesus. With His love, blood, and wisdom's guidance, you will never be lost or forsaken in these things." As I came out of this vision, I was genuinely stunned. I could not wait to understand these insights and begin to apply them. It is truly amazing how much we still have yet to uncover about all God has created.

Chapter 3
Foundations of the Blueprints of Destiny

When trying to press into Heaven on May 5th, 2022, the Holy Spirit said, "Take your time to see, go slowly, and describe what you're looking at." First, I looked down towards the floor. I could see that I was wearing white robes, the outline of clear white illuminated light around my feet. I could sense the light was the appearance of my spirit body. I saw a long staircase of white marble steps before me, ascending upward through what looked like a celestial tunnel. On either side of the stairs were golden handrails, and as I walked up the staircase, I noticed stars, galaxies, planets, streaks of lightning, and bolts of energy. These celestial objects circulated around and throughout this tunnel, much like the event horizon of a black hole. At the end of the tunnel was a bright white light that was circling its outermost edge. I walked up the staircase, and as my head came out on the other side, I could see the radiant beauty of Heaven.

The view was gorgeous and majestic, with snowcapped mountain ranges in the distance. At the foothills of the mountains, there appeared to be cottages, rolling hills of lush green grass, and flowers in all different colors. A long winding path navigated around the hills towards the mountains. In the distance, I could see a body of water, and before it was dozens of beautiful, majestic pine trees. I turned around as I felt the nudge of something on my back. It was a horse named Daphne. I learned that Daphne is an angel assigned to assist me in the realms of Heaven; her appearance, however, was that of a sorrel horse with white spots, a reddish mane, and wings.

"Daphne, what do you have for me today," I asked. A scroll then materialized in my hand. On one side of the scroll was a series of drawings that looked like the blueprints an architect would use; on the opposite side, this scroll appeared like a map.

I noticed two men in white nearby; their names were Stewart and Dana. They said, "The road you're traveling is not the beaten path. This map will direct your steps, and the blueprints will show you the design for Father's best in this season of your life. Worry not about the things ahead, for Heaven provides for all your needs. Let this be a day of soaking in all Heaven has for you!"

Chapter 4
Revelation of Destiny Scrolls

As I stepped into Heaven on another morning, I requested access to the Business Complex. I could see pine trees like green fencing lining the path to the front entrance. I could sense and feel that I had been here before and was reminded of a dream I had years earlier where I was in Heaven and in this place.

As I stepped into the complex, I was greeted by Gloria, a woman in white assigned to me. She then greeted me and remarked that she was happy to see me stepping in for revelation and reminded me of a book I am to write. I had asked for clarity and education on scrolls from a scribe, and Enoch appeared. He greeted me as we had encountered each other a few times prior and began explaining about different types of scrolls. I stopped him and asked, "How do we interact and interpret Destiny Scrolls for businesses?"

Destiny Scrolls

Enoch said, "Destiny Scrolls are the Father's hopes, dreams, and desires for a thing—a business, a person, or a ministry. It is the maximum fulfillment of all that entity can and should aspire to be; it is everything that is good, holy, and pure because it comes from the Father's heart for His children and contains the frequency of love."

He continued, "Destiny Scrolls are like guideposts for the saints; they can map out how Heaven sees a thing and how it could be built out. When following a Destiny Scroll, the best version of something can be achieved because it is the Father's will and His plan for that entity. To interact with a Destiny Scroll, peer into it, step into it, and investigate the hidden treasures within."

As Enoch said this, I could see a series of caves, and it was as if I was walking inside one. I could see mounds of gold and gems inside; I could see ideas for inventions, pathways to new schools of thought and tools called the "Building Blocks of Destiny."

Asking what those were, I was told, "These are desires and intentions. When the saints surrender their plans and submit their will to the Father, His desire and intention for their lives or business can be made manifest. This is a form of submission and surrender to His divine will. This is the place of laying on the altar and allowing your flesh to be in submission to the spirit—this is spirit first living. When you submit to the Father's plans, all things will go well and work out for the good of those who love God. By contrast, when the saints abandon the opportunity to submit to Heaven's plans and decide upon their own course of action, often, this can divert their ability to cultivate the resources the Destiny Scroll would otherwise yield. The desire and intention of Fathers' heart are circumvented by the desire of one's own soul. This motivation many businesses and individuals follow can get them into a place that feels fruitless, dry, or empty because it does not have the grace needed for the venture or task at hand. Many businesses struggle or fail within the first five years because of this common error."

I asked, "So, by better understanding and following the Destiny Scroll as a guide, our client's businesses will have better longevity and business outcomes?" I was told that is correct. I then asked, "If one is already invested based on their own soul's desires, how do we get them back on track?"

Gloria laughed, and Enoch said, "That part is easy—just repent and invite the Father back into the business. Take advantage of the simplicity of the Mercy Court and repent with the clients for where they did not consult or engage Heaven's plan, then go to the Court of Times and Seasons and have their clocks reset.

"Afterward, deeding the territory of the business to Father and inviting Him to be the CEO is in good order. Allow the business owners to submit to stewardship according to Heaven's plans. These are the best steps to move in the right direction. Once this is completed, you can go and look at their Destiny Scrolls and help them to discern what the next step is and should be."

Business Blueprints

I was also shown business blueprints and was told these are quantum maps of how a business will look in any place in time. They can be used in conjunction with the Destiny Scroll to ensure plans are being mapped out and executed correctly.

Commissioning Angels

You may also commission your angels to map out and carry out the plans on the Destiny Scrolls and blueprints to ensure seamless replication of Father's desires for that which you are engaging.

In a subsequent engagement, I learned more on the subject: The Scroll of Life & Times. I was pressing in to hear from Heaven and heard Phillip, my angel, speaking. He said, "All people are given gifts; some choose to use them to advance the Kingdom (of God), others prefer to advance the world, and still others choose to advance their agendas, but all are given by the greatest gift giver of all, God the Father.

"Gifts are wonderful things, but who you choose to use them to serve is most important. Will you choose to serve yourself or to serve others? Will you choose to horde them or multiply them?

"Think of the parable of the talents. There were those servants who made wise investments and those who were stingy and lazy and chose not to invest their talents wisely; choose wisely. As you steward the gifts you have been given wisely, more will be given to you."

I remarked, "You are not just talking about physical gifting, are you?" Phillip said, "No, child of God, I am talking about the law of stewardship of all things—gifts and resources alike."

Suddenly, I could see we were in the Throne Room. Before the throne were three chests—one open and two closed. I noticed the Sea of Glass, like crystal, was like a flowing stream, the most beautiful teal blue and babbling like a brook. As I approached, I heard the Father say, "Beloved, this is a season of rest for you, it is a season of growth, depth of intimacy, and preparing of the way for what comes next."

As I heard these words, I could feel an excitement within my heart, like I was ready to explode with joy.

As I walked over to the open chest before me, I peered into it and saw infant clothes: one blue set, one pink set, onesies, booties, and bonnets. Suddenly, the colors changed to two blue sets, then two pink. I needed clarification as to the color change. I said, Father, what is the meaning of this?

He said, "This part of your scroll had not been written yet." I was baffled as I believed things to be laid out since the beginning of time; however, I have come to understand that there is a Scroll of Life and Times, which differs from the Scroll of Times and Seasons.

The Scroll of Times and Seasons is the Father's perfect will for our lives and destinies. The Scroll of Life and Times, however, is a chronology of the choices we make of our own will and the path we choose for ourselves on Earth.

This is where we can make choices that may divert us from the set course Father would have us walk upon. We make these choices of self-will, out of our choosing or our heart's desire. I had asked, "So, having a vasectomy was not Father's choice for my life?"

I heard, "No, My son. You chose to make that choice out of love and nobility for the one you care for. However, due to that choice, a new timeline has been formed, and you have set the course on this new timeline, nullifying the old one. This portion of life and times is unwritten because your next step or choice is yet unfulfilled."

The Father's command is always to be fruitful and multiply; therefore, He will bless those who choose to do so, and He will also bless those whose choice is not to do so because He loves all His children and wants their utmost joy and contentment.

I asked if this plays into how evil timelines are established, and I was told it is. I asked how the Destiny Scroll works in the mix and was told the Scrolls of Times and Seasons are just for times or seasons, but the Destiny Scroll is from beginning to end and through all eternity.

I then commissioned my angels to the task of ensuring my life and times line up with my Destiny Scroll and times and seasons by helping me to know the choices to make according to Father's will.

I looked in the chest again and saw the color changing stop on double pink. I heard Father say, "The choice is yours, but my heart is always for you to be fruitful and multiply."

Chapter 5
Perfectly Laid Plans

I began to inquire more intently about how Blueprints and Destiny Scrolls could be utilized. It was revealed to me that they are pieces of a puzzle that fit together and can help one return to the Lord's perfect path. I then heard the Holy Spirit speak and postured myself in stillness to receive. He said, "The Father's plans are perfectly laid and intricate. His plans cannot be overcome or circumvented, but every outcome is foreseen." As I was trying to understand this better, I entered a vision of a well-lit pathway. I heard Holy Spirit say, "This is the perfect path, Father's perfect will; there has only been one who followed this path, that one was Jesus."

As I saw and heard these things, I noticed a place of divergence in the perfect pathway. I saw little light paths that protruded out to the right and the left out of the initial way. Some points connected with the "perfect path" laid out in the center and, at other points, diverged again. Different paths were present; they were offshoots but didn't reconnect to the origin. I marveled at this sight as it reminded me of looking at the veins on the leaf of a tree and how intricate the details that are woven into it. I heard Heaven say, "The Father has woven all possible outcomes into the Scroll of Destiny. He knows all the choices and decisions we will make. The Lord orders our steps, but he also keeps track of the steps we order for ourselves. All things work for His good purposes. Destinies may diverge, but always return to His desired plan for His children as time is in His hands."

As I was understanding this with my spirit man, I saw my timeline. In this timeline, my former spouse was chosen of my will, which ended because it wasn't God's perfect will. Simultaneously, I could see my wife's timeline and where things diverged with her former spouse and marriage. Then I could see how the Father had woven our paths together, continuing our destinies, and how we were searching out, walking His path in unison. I heard Him say, "This was destined; there were no mistakes." He said, "Each life born of you both was intended since the beginning of time. This blending is unique, and its pattern is interwoven with the utmost care to provide a future and a hope." I was reminded of Romans 8:28:

> *All things work together for the good of those who love God and are called according to His purposes! (Romans 8:28) (TLV)*

Again, I heard Holy Spirit speaking; He said, "If you seek Him with your whole heart, He will make His plans manifest.

If you don't, He will still make His plans manifest because He loves you. He is a good, good Father. All time is in His hands; fear no evil, for I am with you!"

Chapter 6
Stars, Destinies, and Trade Routes

In another engagement, Heaven showed me an image relating to an encounter that I had had earlier in the day. In this encounter, the ministry team at Heaven Down Business was given a piece of paper that unfolded like a map. This paper looked like a combination of information. It had trade routes, blueprints, and star charts. It depicted necessary information regarding connections, plans, and points of interaction between the business, staff, clients, and those who are yet to come alongside that business.

I was joined in the conference room by Mandy (a woman in white who tended to Heaven Down Business), Frequency, Mack, and Breakthrough, the angels assigned to this entity. Jesus, Matthew, and Abraham had also joined us. "What can you tell me about this paper, its information, and its relevance," I asked. The Lord said, "There is much to know and digest; buckle up." Matthew stood up and started writing on the whiteboard. I could see he was drawing an image of the star charts but also drawing pathways in another color.

I then heard Him explain that stars are sources of trade. They bear resources that can be utilized or traded for business and are power sources for the destinies of individuals and entities. Their placement at the time of the creation of a life influences the gifting and potential one can realize, and they are hosts of Heaven. Stars can be engaged within a fashion of co-laboring between your angels, commissioning, and calling upon them to be plugged into your business from a Heavenly standpoint. When the enemy captures a star, the flow of its resources and benefits of its trade into an entity is halted or polluted. This is an illegal and profane activity of hell that can swiftly be dealt with by accessing the celestial court, much like one would in dealing with fragmentation. The resources traded and provided by one's star can change based on times, seasons, and positioning that would give specific sustenance and equipping based on what is necessary at that moment.

The resources of one's stars are of maximum benefit, specifically within their spheres of influence. However, trade routes exist between stars and entities. This is how things can be traded and stewarded from the Heavenly realm.

Trading into the saints and, therefore, building the Kingdom of God upon the earth is an activity of the hosts of Heaven. The resources traded could be blessings, gifting, jewels, gold, silver, wisdom, and the like. These riches are transported along Heavenly trade routes with assignments to reach an expected destination. The commissioning of angels is highly useful to guard and watch over the provision that has been released.

I asked Heaven, how does one's destiny align with these resources? I heard Heaven say, "The Father's will from the time of our creation, conception, birth, and ultimately relocation to Heaven, orders our steps. We have assignments embedded within the stars. That which is the Father's greatest desire for us to inherit and benefit from can be released through trade routes and acquired from the power source of plugging into our stars. It is the Father's desire for us to come into a greater awareness of the role these entities have in our destiny. This can only be achieved by fully connecting with the Father's heart and submitting to His perfect will. Should we choose our own path, we could choose a way that was not in line with His destiny for our lives. Thus causing some possible reroutes and road hazards along our path from wrong alignments." After this final instruction, the encounter was over.

Chapter 7
Intertwining of Blueprints, Destiny Scrolls, Star Maps, and Trade Routes

On my next adventure into the Heavenly realm, I decided to investigate my blueprints and Destiny Scrolls. I entered into the Business Complex of Heaven and requested an audience with my Heavenly business team. We assembled in a conference room, with a large table before us. I gazed at a document that had been unrolled on this table and realized I was looking at Heaven's blueprint for my businesses and ministries. As I observed the layout and intricate details, I noticed this was both an outline and architecture of structures that would be operated under my stewardship. I could see seven different structures on this blueprint, and as I looked on, some angels came up and overlaid a Destiny Scroll over the blueprint. As they set it down, the information on the Destiny Scroll interacted with the blueprints' designs. These objects came alive, filling in the finite details. I began to see information appear that described each structure, how it operated, what it produced, what type of entity it was, how it was to be built out, and what Father's plan was for these things.

As I glanced up above the table, I noticed a holographic projection that had started to appear. Inquiring what this additional information was, Heaven responded that it was, "star maps." My spirit man immediately understood that our stars were power sources connected by trade routes. These trade routes were superhighways that Heaven used to get supplies and resources to all of my structures. Looking down at the Destiny Scroll and blueprints on the table, I noticed a space between them. Suspended in the air, I could see the star maps populating information, which moved and interacted with the Destiny Scrolls and blueprints. The star maps started to interact with the information on the table. Clear cylindrical pipes appeared, resembling pneumatic tube systems. They transported resources, like one may see vacuum tubes used in a bank to send deposits through.

Heaven said, "These are trade routes, portals, and wormholes. They are points of transportation by which provision flows from Heaven down into the earth." I had heard the Holy Spirit speak and say, "These things work together for the good of those who love God, His sons; for those who have chosen with the intention of their will to serve Him unreservedly and do what is good in His eyes. Those who operate in wickedness, their portion shall be cut off. Their trade routes shall be blocked. The work and labor of their hands shall be cursed. Their field shall not bear fruit, but those who honor the Lord with their hearts, lips, first fruits, and their offerings will flourish. They shall be trees in Lebanon, their vats shall overflow, and their households shall never be lacking, no matter how things look. The nature of the Lord will always be supernatural; the covenant God has with His sons is irrevocable; nothing can stop what the Lord has released." (Deuteronomy 28)

The Holy Spirit continued, "Child of God, do not be afraid, do not allow the lies of the enemy to distract you from creating what the Kingdom has intended for you to build, do not let the enemy strike fear in your heart, and keep you from working in the fields. The Father has given to you, so do not allow laziness or perversity to creep his way in and derail you or your generations from receiving the fullness of your true inheritance. The Father is well pleased with you. He's well pleased with your tenacity, hunger for more, and desire to do what has been put in your heart. As you continue to put Him first place in your life, you will see even greater wonders than you have already beheld."

Suddenly, I was standing on what looked like a city street and noticed the block I was standing on looked decrepit. I saw horse-drawn chariots in the street; noticeably, there were portals over this area, but they looked as if they had been blocked. Holy Spirit said, "What you see here in the natural is the evidence of God, the society of soul rule decision, where sin not only glorifies the world but is celebrated. Natural eyes would notice a place filled with sin to appear as if a film of dirt was upon it. It appears to have no peace in regions not built according to the Father's plans." I could tell His plane of existence was nowhere on the earth; however, it had striking similarities to some of the most impoverished neighborhoods I had seen in major US cities.

Next, I was transported outside of a beautiful city. In the midst of it, there were structures that looked like the towers of a castle. The glass radiated off the buildings like the brightest crystal in a serial golden glow around this place. I could see joyful people on the streets, greeting one another, engaging in trade, smiling and laughing. There was no hurt or bitterness and no fleshly emotion. I was told these are the trading forces of Heaven when operating according to the Father's plans. This is how things turn out pristine and beautiful, flourishing like an empire going through a golden age. I was told the choice was ours to make; no one will force us to build according to Heaven's plan, and we should choose wisely.

Many are the afflictions of the righteous, but the LORD delivers him out of them all. (Psalm 34:19) (NIV)

Mountains

At this point, my brain had been overloaded with new revelation. I needed to reassure my soul that it did not need to be a gatekeeper, as my spirit could understand these new revelations. I asked Heaven to help me understand how our mountains line up in relation to the heavenly resources and destinations at our disposal. I wanted to know how to fully connect Destiny Scrolls, blueprints, star maps, trade routes, and the positioning of our stars to these structures. I was taken into a vision and shown that our mountains are a position of authority in the second Heaven. The Holy Spirit explained, "It is a place of rest, a storehouse of heavenly resources, and a positioning by which we rule, reign, and judge principalities, powers of wickedness, and their dominions."

I asked why I wanted to be in the second Heaven, and not in the third? I was shown the interconnectedness of these pathways. Heaven explained that our mountains function as outposts and storehouses in the 2nd Heaven. Resources flow from Heaven down through our stars, into our mountains, and then they can be pulled down into our assignments into the earth. They are pulled down through prayer, declarations of faith, spiritual warfare, and other activities we have long engaged in but have not unpacked the process.

I was shown in my life that this positioning had been neglected. By vacating that place of authority, I was leaving it exposed for something else to take its place on my throne. I saw how our mountains are connected, as well as the flow of the trade routes between these Heavenly places. Holy

Spirit revealed how sons can flow with Heaven to occupy and steward.

The analogy I was given also related to the revelation of blueprints, Destiny Scrolls, trade routes, and star maps. I have broken each one down right below:

- **Blueprints** are like the foundations of a house.
- **Destiny Scrolls** define the structures we are to oversee and operate.
- **The Trade Routes** are portals/gates/wormholes; in essence, they would be like the wires in the wall or pipes that bring electricity or water into a house; they transmit resources.
- **The Star Maps** show how and where our stars receive the resources from Heaven that flow through our mountains and into the earth to build the Kingdom, ministries, and businesses.

Looking in the spirit, I could see my stars above my mountain. The stars were in a mobile positioning, meaning from them, I could move about in this realm through time and space, where my mountain was stationary. From within the mountain, I was shielded in the citadel of the Lord, with many Heavenly resources, rooms, treasuries, and other places to explore. Inside was a place of safety and security from outside influences. At the top was a throne, a place of rest that sat on an elevator-like platform, which could carry me into my star. From there, it could go up again into the throne room to set me in my position at the Father's right hand as a son, along with Christ.

It is important to note that we need to control and occupy our mountains, in Godly authority, to steward resources properly and ensure that the enemy and his forces do not turn to evil, the things the Lord God intended for good.

Chapter 8
The Tunnel of Time

One spring morning, I awoke to hear the Lord speaking to me. He said, *"Open your eyes and look towards Heaven."*

I saw Jesus, riding on a cloud, coming towards me. He reached out His hand and lifted me onto it. As I sat next to Him, He said, *"Come let me show you what is happening in the heavens right now."*

The cloud took off at light speed like a rocket. I could see video screens beneath us, all in a row, tuned to what would be considered many different channels. Each one represented a different point in time and a different timeline. The Lord said that these were times and seasons. We sped above them. Just ahead, I could see that we were headed towards a tunnel; I heard Him say, "You're entering the tunnel of time; this is a place that spans the times and seasons of your life."

When we entered this tunnel, I saw that it started at one point as a straight line. Upon the line, I noticed various other points. At specific points, other lines broke out and diverged to the right or the left onto various other paths. Meanwhile, other points on those paths had lines divided into other branches. From the alternate points and paths, lines at various moments entered back onto the initial path. They continued to another point, and again, there were splits in these paths. The lines would diverge off to the right or left and then at another point would divide again, branch off, and stop. Other lines had fewer complex pathways that would loop back to that main line or split off at a midpoint. I noticed that some of the lines that had broken off from the main pathway returned to the main line and converged at a center point. Holy Spirit said that this was the point of salvation in my life. The multitudes of branches I had seen were the moments where I had made personal choices of self-will as opposed to God's will. These were places where my foot went to the right or left as I diverged from the path of wisdom. In some instances, I found a way back to the right path, only to make the same mistakes over and over till the point of surrender and salvation. After the point of salvation, I noticed the same pattern of coming to a point and lines diverging to the left or right. As the main points on the center line continued, I saw the divergences became fewer and farther between. Holy Spirit explained, "This was the path of maturing in the spirit, learning to be a son, walk as a son, and operate as a son." In doing so, I was engaging Heaven, receiving wisdom, and yielding to more of the Lord's perfect will for my life as opposed to choices of self-will.

I was reminded of the teaching on maps, times, and timelines. How, in commissioning my angels, I could ask them to go into the maps of times and timelines to remove the parts of time where I was out of alignment with Father's will. I called my angels to come near and remove where I had been out of alignment with Papa's will. I commissioned them to reconnect time and blot out the areas that diverged from Father's best. Immediately, I started seeing the branches disappearing and consolidating into the main timeline. In this process, I realized the tunnel of time was a spherical place, and the lines of time were cyclical and curved.

I then saw the room shift to the right. I could see older variations of the timeline at that point. Branches split off from the main line that weren't visible in the previous view of the dimensional timeline. I knew that these were timeline divergences in other dimensions.

I again commissioned my angels to blot out the instances where I was out of alignment with Father's will "in and out of time; and in every timeline, age, realm, and dimension." I could then see those lines consolidating back to the main branch. The Lord said that this is the work of the amendment of in time and out of time, and he encouraged me to continue to use it well. He wants us to be mindful that there is more than one dimension and realm to be fighting the good fight of faith in. The enemy plays illegally and unfairly; he cheats and doesn't play by the rules. These tools will equip you to overcome unseen things and have profound effects as they are engaged. He said, "Carry on, little soldier," and softly patted me on the head. We took off on the cloud towards a gate of light, and I could feel the presence of unexplainable resounding peace washing over me as we flew off into this new place.

Chapter 9
Time Angels & Time Gates

As I entered prayer, I felt the need to enter the Court of Times and Seasons. I knew in my spirit that there was a need for divine alignment of my family's times and seasons. As I entered this court, I saw two angels standing on either side of the judge's bench. I had never seen this class of angel before in this courtroom. They were very tall, wearing gold head gear that had a wing on each side over where the ears would be. There was an opening for the face areas, but the rest of the head was encased in gold. They appeared to be wearing bright orange and gold garments; each had a golden staff. At the top end and bottom end of the staff were golden hourglasses. They had gleaming white sand inside. Holy Spirit informed me that these were known as time angels or timekeeper angels, assigned to patrol the realms of all time.

As I prayed and repented in this court based on my family's need, I was instructed to ask for a time realignment. I saw angels tap the bottoms of their staffs on the ground three times in unison. Then they swung toward each other as if they were jousting. The shafts of gold clanged together to form an X shape; a gateway opened. The Just Judge spoke and said that this was called the Gate of Time. This gate was opened to realign time, both in and out of time. I understood this was a key to include with the use of other Heavenly tools, such as capture bags and amendments of in time and out of time when seeking justice in the Courts of Heaven.

Sands of Time and Cycles of Time

In another engagement, I was brought into the Court of Favor. I saw golden gates open, and as I walked through them, I found myself outside in a courtyard setting. There were many people in white linen gathered there. I noticed a cobblestone floor with darker-colored stones circling the center of this courtyard. In the center was the appearance of colored gemstones and gold, forming the shape of a crown. I saw a throne in the midst and felt the conviction of the Holy Spirit instructing me to invite the Lord to sit on the throne of my heart.

Afterward, I saw a plum-colored armchair covered in velvet. It had been placed for me to sit in and marvel at the beauty of the Lord. I asked where I was and heard Heaven say, "You are in the mountain of God, the place of my being, my innermost thoughts within my heart.". As I looked around, I noticed waterfalls of translucent gold water pouring down around me. There was a narrow pathway of gold stones covered partially with golden sand. A gleaming white hourglass at one end of the path kept turning, but no sand fell on either end. It was called the Sands of Time. The sand inside was filled on both top and bottom but never moved in a decreasing or increasing way in either bulb. It was whiter than any earthly white, almost blinding in color.

I asked what the significance of the sand was. Heaven said, "There is no construct or time in this ethereal and eternal realm. Eternity is from everlasting to everlasting. In Heaven/Him, there is no aging, no feeling of 'being pressed for time,' no reason to strive. As a son, the yielding and entering eternity, through the door that is the Lamb of God, will allow you to draw upon Heavenly resources for all parts of your destiny." As I heard this, I could see what appeared to be fragments of a mirror. The reflecting pieces were purple and swirled around, lying next to one another to form an image, like pieces of a puzzle when put together.

These fragments depict all the pieces of your destiny, every step, every mission, and every assignment. When put together, they weave the tapestry of your divine timeline and traverse the course of your Destiny Scroll. In eternity, there are no mistakes or setbacks. Only opportunities exist to seize the wisdom, plans, and blueprints required to accomplish these goals. As I tried to wrap my head around this, I asked Father for counsel, as my mind was having trouble understanding.

A man in white named Mitchell approached; I had met him before. We greeted one another, and I asked for assistance in understanding this. He instructed me to tell my soul to be at rest, even go to sleep, for it was the part of me that was resisting 'comprehensive capacity.' I prayed for my spirit to be forward and my soul to be at rest. After repositioning, Mitchell began to teach me.

He said, "Think of these pieces as waypoints on a journey, checkpoints if you will. Each checkpoint is marked off on a map, signifying the when and where. There is something you are destined to experience or a person that you are supposed to interact with. Every point connects to another point; however, in Heaven, time is cyclical not linear. No two points intersect on a timeline from the earthly standpoint. However, in Heaven, all points connect to each other point. If you recall the teaching from Dr. Ron Horner's revelation on maps, time, and timelines, you will recall the maps they had seen were not linear. They were more like spheres, almost like a depiction of Ezekiel's wheels within wheels, heavenly maps. In Father's will for His children, there are no missed opportunities, just things we have not interacted with 'yet.' There is always a new season or new opportunity that aligns perfectly with your Destiny Scroll. Even after one gains the heavenly body or ceases to be on the earth, there is still more of their destiny that plays out in Heaven. Everyone has a part to play in the grand scheme of the Father's ethereal architecture of the universe and the Heavens."

I could see what looked like the known universe and even distant star systems that hadn't been discovered. Also, those that would never be discovered by humans on Earth. Wrapping around them was Heaven; the layout looked spherical in nature. Heaven is all around everything. The only way I could comprehend it was to think of it like a Tootsie Roll pop. The 2nd Heaven, a galactic plane, was like the tootsie roll center. The earth was like the stick in the middle, and Heaven was like the candy shell, encapsulating everything.

Mitchell could see this perplexed me; he said, "I think that is enough for today; just know that no opportunity is missed or lost. What you cannot do in this season will come about in another. Use that to assist you in resting in the Father's presence and to keep you from crossing the boundary into striving. Striving produces weariness; rest produces fruit!

Ancient of Days Encounter

In my prayer time, on the morning of December 17th, 2022, when I pressed into Heaven, I went into the Court of Wisdom and sat upon a comfy red velvet chair to read the word. I heard "Daniel seven" in my spirit, and as I came to verse nine, the revelation of the Ancient of Days opened to me. The Lord showed me the beginning when Heaven was all that existed. I saw the moment when God spoke all creation into existence. The Ancient of Days was present, seated on the throne, in His courts, executing justice as books were opened and presented.

I had heard in the spirit:

This is a season of learning for you. I want to teach you great and wonderful things, but you must keep quiet about them till the appointed time. This will be a season of maturity.

Be wise of the enemy's tactics; as your wife moves forth to train herself, the enemy will show His hand. You will see an uptick in activity, first trying to manifest in the children and then other external situations. You are to be still and keep your peace, for these are not to throw you from your course, but they are to distract your wife from hers. As the fire increases and burns white hot, the purification process will be completed in you and your generations in this season and give birth to what is to come next.

Steward My fire, soak in My presence, and let the love of My son's sacrifice drip like sweet honey from your lips. Let the dew of Heaven give life to those around you who are lost in darkness and hopelessness. Keep your wick trimmed and your lamp filled with oil. The days of the Lord are yet at hand, and soon, all will know the eminence of My presence.

I asked to see my Scrolls of Destiny and was taken to the Courts of Destiny. In this place, there were tables that had square cubby holes placed on them, each with a scroll; and there were aisles of these tables. We were led to a place by the angel Gabriel; he pulled up the scroll, cracked its seal, and began to read it.

He began in the 23rd year of the 2000 era; on Earth, there will be much turmoil, but in your house, you shall have peace. You will be a peacekeeping vessel bringing many to know, see, and believe the promises of God and His seed. It will be a year of expansion, rapid promotion, evolution, and decaying of old mindsets and paradigms for you and your family. Your tribe shall flourish and expand, and it shall expand a second and third time in the coming era. Time is futile and fleeting, so do not let it be wasted. Be proactive, laboring to enter the Father's rest, only administrating tasks from eternity. {He paused and paraphrased} This means entering into His rest and engaging Heaven more and more each day.

Your inheritance is great, but your role as a son is greater. Step into the newness of this season. As a prophetic action, I stood up, took a physical step forward, and declared by faith the door to the old was now shut.

Discerning Times & Seasons

On another occasion, my adventures in Heaven started standing on a cliff overlooking a great chasm. Daphne appeared and instructed me to climb on her back. I began to look around at the vast scenery. I could see the valleys below and a castle in the distance. Daphne took three large gallops, and before I could blink, we were atop the castle on the balcony of the tallest spire. I could see all this region of Heaven from this vantage point. As I walked into the spire, there was a throne room. I could see the Father on the throne, the lampstands, and four living creatures before it, as depicted in the fourth chapter of Revelation. Jesus was standing there, and He warmly embraced me. Father spoke and said:

> *My son, I am so proud of the man that you are and all that you have accomplished. Never let up in your pursuit of all things that are righteousness.*
>
> *The disconnection from your surroundings you are feeling is the grace being lifted. This will be apparent as you near the end of certain assignments in your life. You will know the time by the ease and grace lifting. Be sure to enjoy what you're in the midst of,*

even if it is not as colorful as it was when your assignment first came in season. Think of the leaves on the trees during an assignment season; they are lush and green, but when the grace has lifted and their assigned season is over, they turn brown and fall from the branches.

Quantum Shifts

During my next encounter with Heaven, I was brought into a room I had never seen before. It was explained to me as the room of quantum time shifts. I knew in here I could skip ahead in my times and seasons, but I desired not to skip past this process of pruning, death, and coming into deeper intimacy. I had been asking the Father about intimacy and deepening intimacy, so it was no surprise when suddenly I saw many people from the cloud of witnesses who walked closely with God. I was introduced to Joan of Arc, St. Francis of Assisi, and others who talked to me about love. Enoch approached, and he described some of His walk with the Lord. He told me that the evil grip on the earth today was different and more prevalent than how things had been in His day, pulling one to and fro.

As he talked, I cried out to the Father that I wanted to know Him deeper in love. I wanted to know His essence, grace, mercy, and wisdom. Then I asked Him to help me know Him as love; I saw Jesus being nailed to the cross. As they hammered in the nails, He cried out, "This is for you, Jeremy Friedman." I cried and asked, "Why, Lord?" He said, "Because you are the one whom I love, this is for you. You are My chosen vessel, and from you will come generations." He also said, "From you, many have already been saved and delivered, and many more will be." I could hear Him say that I don't need the word of a prophet or a man, for they will never understand me, my walk, or my path. The voice of the Lord alone will guide me. As I heard this, the Father grabbed my hand, and as a little boy, I walked with Him down a golden path with rubies as the rocks aligned to its edges. The Lord said I must choose a path; the one ahead would be more difficult but rewarding, with the fullness of all God wanted for me. The path to the left would be the one I had been on. I would see many signs and wonders, but it would not be His choice for me; I said, "Father, I want your best."

When I said that, I could see we were in Safehouse Church. I saw myself on the altar face down, crying out to God. This was February 2022; He said this was when I gave Him my "yes."

Flash forward to October 2022; I could see myself face down on the altar with half of my family again. The view skipped again to June 2023, where my whole family and others were all there face down on the altar. This time, I could see the throne of God in front of the church. We were all in white, and our crowns were laid out before us. Many angels attended to us, and I could see men and women in white moving about in the heavenly realm, praying for all and speaking to those there. As this continued, I stood with Jesus watching. He was watching intently when suddenly a woman, a mother, jumped up, screaming that she had been healed. Everyone screamed hallelujah and gave glory to God.

Afterward, we returned to our faces on the altar and did not get up. The Lord said, "This is the season where you will learn to remain on my altar. The hustle and bustle of everyday life and the cares of this world will no longer affect you. I am taking you out of the world, and I am taking the world out of you. In June, I asked if you would give me all of you, and in July, I asked if you would give me a year and sit at my table. This is your inheritance to walk as these (meaning Enoch and the others who were martyred or sacrificed for intimacy with the Lord)." Jesus continued saying, "The trials and tests would be great, but the reward that awaits you is far greater. He said, "You are not a failure; you are My greatest success."

Chapter 10
The Frequencies of Heavenly Healing

On the morning of February 8th, 2022, I found myself walking down a stairway in Heaven. The steps were constructed from a cascading waterfall. As I came to the bottom step, I stepped off onto a platform that looked like ice. It was the sea of glass, like crystal, before the throne of the Lord. I was in the throne room, and as soon as I stepped down, I heard the Holy Spirit speak to me. I heard, "Do not let the weariness of this natural realm overpower and affect you. The frequencies in the airwaves of the region that you are in are overpowering. They can be oppressive for those who do not know how to step out of the natural confines that surround them. In essence, evil frequencies can imprison people. They put hardship on them, like worry, anxiety, and fear, but as you know, those frequencies are not ones you subscribe to. Step up and out into the frequencies of Heaven and allow My peace and joy to overpower you. Let the water of righteousness refill you, and the living Waters flow outward through your belly. Allow these waters to envelope around that which you occupy in the physical realm. You are a supernatural being; therefore your supernatural spirit is enshrouded in glory alone! Instruct your spirit to translate these frequencies from the throne room into your soul and body realm. No matter where you go, external forces will not oppress you, but you will be only filled with joy, peace, and the Father's love for you."

In this instance, I could sense what felt like waves, not those of water, but waves of peace going through the atmosphere. They were going through me and calming my being. The peace washed over me like waves rolling onto the seashore and then out again. Suddenly, the scene changed; I saw white sand and a row of palm trees. I felt warmth and heard the sound of seagulls and children giggling; I looked to my left and saw Jesus walking down the seashore, coming towards me. With each step, I could feel the thunderous beauty of His love and peace; it overwhelmed, restored, and re-centered me.

The Father said, "I am removing you and your family from this place. This has been a place of healing for you and for your family. It was a place of growth and of forming the foundation for building the next level. You will start to see and feel natural shifts and releases. Keep your eyes open as I move things on this Earth; you will see many mighty wonders in your midst. Salvations and invitations from My Kingdom, even beginning around your birthday, you will feel a greater shifting and quaking than has just been felt. With the anticipation and excitement rising and your expectation increasing, fast and pray, My son, fast and pray!! Your righteous faith is the key to unlocking things that have never been fathomed."

Heaven's Health Center

On another occasion, I was greeted by Daphne and a man in white linen whose name was Francisco. Francisco said I could call him Frank for short. Frank had black hair, a black handlebar mustache, and a pointed Van Gogh goatee. Frank informed me about Heaven's Health Center and brought me to see, understand, and perceive it. Frank explained that Heaven's Health Center has three main areas with various offshoots.

The three main areas cater to the mind (soul), body, and spirit. Everyone in their heavenly body is fit; the health center translates that down via the spirit to the natural realm. Frank explained that the mind area focuses on our thought life. It takes every high-minded thought captive and helps our thoughts translate to those of the Father. This will break off self-limiting and self-depreciating thought forms.

The second area to focus on is the body. The body translates Heaven's frequency of how God created us into a healthy pattern for motivation in exercise, healthy eating, digestion, metabolism, and good stewarding of the bodies God has given us upon the earth. The Body Department in

Heaven's Health Center can also help our bodies on Earth overcome and function with issues that typically occur from unhealthy eating, poor lifestyle choices, and genetic disorders through proper physical alignment with Heaven. Frank had me look at myself and explained in the spirit, everyone is fit; our spirit man does not necessarily reflect how our body looks in the natural and vice versa. In Heaven, we can translate our spiritual physique to natural.

In the Spirit Center, there are spiritual foundations and truths that we can have imparted into the spirit to help translate us into how we are to operate spiritually. There are heavenly realities that have yet to be fully accessed or have been long forgotten on Earth. These include age reversal, transportation, levitation, healing, etc.

Heaven's Health Center has two hallway connections on the left side of the building. There is a connection between Heaven's Hospital and the Healing Gardens. The right side leads to the Business Complex, and on the 2nd floor, there is a connection from the pool to the Salon Department. It was explained that this department's sauna, showers, steam room, and whirlpool are shared by the business complex and the beginning of the Health Center. The gym in the Business Complex and Health Center are part of the same structure.

After this was explained, I declared that I chose with the intention of my will to sign myself and my family into the health complex. We are to receive Heaven's plan for our lives spiritually, physically, and mentally. It is to be reflected in the natural realm in Jesus' name, and I commissioned our angels to assist in translating the spiritual and heavenly realities down to earth with us and in us in Jesus' name.

Healing

As I ventured into another revelatory encounter, I walked across a rainbow bridge over a river of living water. The bridge led to something the Lord called Strawberry Fields. I chuckled and said, "Isn't that a song?" But the field was full of strawberries singing praises to the Lord. It was also full of sunflowers, daisies, dandelions, daffodils, and other beautiful flowers of every kind. There were floating jars present; I saw one full of honey. The Lord told me to take some of it, that it would be sweet in my mouth and bitter in my stomach.

In another jar was oil for healing. The Lord began to expand upon the healing anointing that I possess. He said, "Look at when you started to struggle recently; it was after the word of knowledge and healing miracle you witnessed. There's nothing the enemy hates more than healing. Healing brings hope, stirs up joy and faith, and gives Glory to God. Healers are a threat to the enemy's plan. That is the cause of this trial. Don't look at struggle as a failure; look at it as a test, a stepping stone."

As I started to meditate upon these words, Heaven gave me one final instruction:

Step in, step up, rejoice, and overcome.

When My steps were bathed with cream, and the rock poured out rivers of oil for me! (Job 29:6) (NKJV)

A thousand may fall at your side, ten thousand at your right hand, but it will not come near you. (Psalm 91:7) (NKJV)

Chapter 11
Restoration & Awestruck Wonder

At another time, I was going through some momentary trials. It was one of those times when I felt like curling up and crying. I entered worship broken, empty, weeping, and lying on the floor before the Lord crushed. I heard the Father speak to me and repeat the following:

You are My Lily of the Valley.

You are My Rose of Sharon.

The Holy Spirit told me to open Psalm 34 and read it in the passion translation. As I read it, I wept bitterly and repented of my wayward heart. The following verses reverberated the condition of my heart and reflected the emotional state of my soul.

> *Even the strong and the wealthy grow weak and hungry, but those who passionately pursue the Lord will never lack any good thing. Do you want to live a long, good life, enjoying the beauty that fills each*

day? Then, never speak a lie or allow wicked words to come from your mouth. Keep turning your back on every sin and make 'peace' your life motto. Practice being at peace with everyone.

The Lord sees all we do; he watches over His friends day and night. His godly ones receive the answers they seek whenever they cry out to him. But the Lord has made up His mind to oppose evildoers and to wipe out even the memory of them from the face of the earth. Yet when holy lovers of God cry out to Him with all their hearts, the Lord will hear them and come to rescue them from all their troubles.

The Lord is close to all whose hearts are crushed by pain, and he is always ready to restore the repentant one. Even when bad things happen to the good and godly ones, the Lord will save them and not let them be defeated by what they face. God will be your bodyguard to protect you when trouble is near. Not one bone will be broken. Evil will cause the death of the wicked, for they hate and persecute the devoted lovers of God. Make no mistake about it: God will hold them guilty and punish them; they will pay the penalty! But the Lord has paid for the freedom of His servants, and he will freely pardon those who love him. He will declare them free and innocent when they turn to hide themselves in him. (Psalms 34:10, 12-22) (TPT)

After reading this, I lay on the floor crying out to the Father; I said, "Take me and all I have. I lay myself on your altar as a sacrifice." I went into an encounter in Heaven where I was walking on a path with the Lord. I saw bushes with leaves of ruby sapphire and emerald, and I saw Daphne waiting to carry me away. As we rode on together, I heard the Lord say, "I shall call you Lion-heart" for you have the heart of a lion, the boldness, prestige, and majesty of a king, but the meekness and grace of a dove." We came to a waterfall that stretched out into a stairway that led down into a cave. I heard the Holy Spirit say, "this was the cave of wonders, it was a secret place, a place of awe and wonder to marvel at the beauty of the Lord, a place of restoration to restore childlike innocence that had been lost and the awestruck wonder of a child's heart to the Father."

Suddenly, we were in the throne room, and the Father was spinning me around dancing. I could see the earth below and all the planets, stars, and galaxies. All around were the angels, a cloud of witnesses, and those in Heaven before the throne. He spun me around as we danced in the most glorious ballroom. He said, "You are so beautiful; even on what you think is your worst day, I still love you. I still adore you." Suddenly, I noticed it wasn't just me, but me, my wife, kids, and all my descendants dancing with the Father. He said, "Let My love be the thing that propels you forward in life, the reward you seek."

Ascending to New Height

On my next plunge into the realm of the spirit, I was swimming in a sea. I could see fish of many varieties, and when I surfaced, there was a beach with a message and keys in a bottle. I noticed that the message said, "Hall of Treasures," and there was a key with it that belonged to a specific treasure chest. Inside the bottle was a giant white feather with black on the tip. I heard the Lord say,

> *You are ascending to new heights, and the embattlements and embargoes you have faced are just the opposition before the new level. The strategies of Satan are to woo you with the world, to distract you with even your blessings, so your focus is shifted from the Father's face. Grace to you, My son, press into My word and let it be a lamp unto your feet to light your path.*

The Father spoke and said,

> *To be strong in me means to rest in the power of My might and strength. You will succeed and prevail by My power and strength, for I do not tire or grow weary. Your enemies will be put asunder, and the*

powers of hell will be shut down. They will be bound at the sound of your voice; your steps will be bathed in butter and oil. Revelations will flow like streams in the Negev if you heed My instruction, listen to My voice, obey My statutes, and observe the ordinances I give you.

He continued saying,

To enter the new season and possess the gate, you must leave behind the barren wasteland of the world. Those closest to you, even your children, will fight and oppose you as you develop an extreme distaste and hatred for the profane things of this world. Fear not, little flock, for My word is truth.

Your children will experience me and experience deliverance, but they must choose their own way. Do you not suppose that some of what you think is an onslaught of the enemy is really me exposing that which needs to die and be pruned off lives? Did you not consider getting rid of the root of frustration? I will expose that which has been hidden till all submit to My ways. Fear not, beloved, for I am with you and will resist your pride. I will tear down what does not belong in My house for you, My son, are My holy mountain!

Chapter 12
Father's Garden

As I walked in a garden with the Father, I asked what He had to tell me this day. He said:

My child, you don't need to earn your stripes. Remember, you were bought with a price; you were chosen. I want you to rest in this season; rest in Me; rest in My presence. Let your countenance, your ambition, and your passion be restored. Let the busyness that has overtaken you become ease and peace. Don't allow the busyness of warfare the enemy had put before you consume your time. Don't let it distract you from Me. How will your lamp get filled with oil if you are too busy to go and be poured out upon? I am well pleased with how you have honored My chosen and anointed ones. I will honor you in My Kingdom for how you have honored others.

Suddenly, I saw a giant sheet cake with countless candles. I asked what the cake was for. I heard, "Because we are celebrating you today. Jeremy, today is the dawning of a new day, a new season, a new step out on the path of your destiny in Christ. Today is a day on which there will be no turning back. The faucets are turned on, the flood gates are open, the chaff will be blown away, the dust removed, the gunk expunged, and every hindrance destroyed. This is so that you may move ahead into the next dimension of your calling, completely free from the past and unhindered to do the Father's will."

I was handed what looked like a mini wheel within a wheel. The Lord told me,

> *This is a watcher. It has been assigned to watch over the new territories you are being given authority and jurisdiction over. Do not underestimate its use by size, for the size is symbolic of the infancy stage of this new territory and call upon your life. There is much to be birthed in your life over the next 20 years; think of this as a sign and a wonder to demonstrate these years of trials and tests at the teething years. The years where you're learning vital developmental Kingdom truths that are needed to mold you into who you are to become. Lean not on your gifting but upon the gift-giver. Wonder not why things don't seem to be free-flowing and seek first the Kingdom of God and the Father's heart. The torrents of refreshment and revelation will be poured*

out in an unstoppable and uncountable measure. You have no lack, dear one. Again, I say, 'YOU HAVE NO LACK, DEAR ONE.'

As I was hearing this, I saw Jesus as the one speaking. The frequency of these words shook me to my core as the magnitude of a lion's roar. I could see crusty, dry places shattering and breaking off of me. They looked like pieces of a broken statue and underneath was fresh new skin. The Lord said, "You are indeed a new wine skin; be filled with new wine."

As I heard this, I was wrestling internally with a desire to run to a prophet to hear a word from the Lord regarding my present circumstances. This had been a season of learning to hear His voice and not rely on a word from a man of God. The Holy Spirit interrupted this internal struggle within my thoughts and said:

Do you need a word? Be filled with sweet new wine; let your drink become the wine of joy and gladness in your belly. As you worship, you will become drunk in the spirit with the love of the Father, which is from everlasting to everlasting.

I obeyed this instruction, worshipped, and wept as His sweet presence overwhelmed and comforted me.

Seed & Authority

Soon after, the Holy Spirit started to download some revelation on how to gain the upper hand in prayer when interceding for situations regarding land, territories, and nations. Heaven said, "If you want authority over something, sow a seed. Don't let the enemy deceive you and make you think that you have come into agreement with the sins of the nation. You have more power than he does to affect change, and you can spoil his plans. If you want to change a geographic place, start praying over your property there." I was told, "When you sow a seed or have ownership of property in a place, you have a stake in it and, therefore, a foothold to ruin his plans and rain on his parade. Wake up to the truth of the power that resides in you through My spirit; let the Holy Ghost be your guide."

This brief encounter helped me embrace the following principle of intercession for other places. If you want greater authority over something, sow a seed into a place, and you will have greater influence when you pray over it.

Field of Dreams

In another engagement, I found myself walking on a snow-covered field. The sky overhead was filled with luminous stars. It looked like the northern lights (the aurora borealis) were streaking across it in their radiant multicolored beauty. I could see a shooting star streak across the sky, and as I walked, I felt the need to invite the spirit of Wisdom to come and walk with me. When Wisdom appeared, she began to speak and said, "This is the field of dreams. What you see is a manifestation of what you dream of seeing, doing, or being able to do in the natural realm." To clarify, I asked, is it essentially a heavenly simulation?

Wisdom replied, "Exactly. It is also a place that will help you to expand the 'muscle' or tools of seeing. Since seeing is using the imagination to draw a picture, this is a safe space of practice to enhance your God-given ability and talent. Many gifted and prophetic artists already access this place when envisioning the concepts they create on physical media. It is a realm of creativity and planning."

As we continued to walk toward the distance, the scene changed into what looked like the inside of a palace throne room. There was a warm, vibrant fire in the fireplace; I saw swords and a shield mounted on one wall with a throne set up. Wisdom informed me that I was now thinking of the Father, so I was transported into this scene. She continued, "As you delve into creativity, you can access this realm as a resource to sketch out, practice, and plan out things one wishes to execute in the natural."

Forest of Truth

Another time, I was taken to a forest called the Forest of Truth. It was full of lush greenery and tall, beautiful trees. I was told the forest of truth is a destination or a starting access point where many gates and portals could be accessed through the Father's truth. I stepped into one that led to the 'place of rest;' it looked much like a private Caribbean island with palm trees, serene, a lounge chair in the sand, and gorgeous blue water. It was described to me that relaxation could be accessed here, much like resting on such a beach in the natural. Next, I was taken to the 'place of access,' like a divine superhighway of light, where light poured out from above. This place gave access to wisdom and knowledge that poured out from the Father to the saint.

Meadow of the Son

Daphne greeted me as I stepped into Heaven on April 26th, 2022. She said, "Hop on; we have much to attend to." Instantly, we were in a realm called 'Meadow of the Son,' it was a green meadow brightly lit by the glory of God. There was lush green grass, many colorful flowers, and children playing and laughing. Jesus was there, and He took me by the hands, happy to see me, and we swung around in circles spinning, like playing ring around the rosy.

The Father was there and grabbed my face and whispered, "I love you." I could feel the atmosphere shift into one of pure joy and delight. In the natural, I was standing at my daughter's bus stop on a drizzly, chilly, grey spring morning, but all I sensed was the beauty of Heaven in the spirit.

I heard Stewart, a man in white linen, proclaim,

This is the dawning of a new day in your life as a son, as a Christian, as a child yielded to hear the voice of the Lord. Expect the Father's goodness and expect the unexpected. Expect that he will never fail or forsake you. Expect deliverance, salvations, new levels of joy, and new encounters with Heaven. Nothing can stop our God; fear and worry can't limit God. Therefore, they cannot limit you; step into the richness of the Father's delight and pleasure to see you walk in the freedom of emotion and thought and the freedom that flows freely from the measure of joy being released on this day.

After I heard these words, I saw a company of seven angels. They had long horns or trumpets with flags on each one. Each flag had one of the seven colors of the rainbow, representing the seven spirits of God. As they blew a thunderous blast, it resounded across all of Heaven, and the physical force of the frequencies of Heaven swept across all that was around and before us. The frequencies ripped like water ripples over mountains, hills, and valleys. As they rippled, the scenery transformed into beautiful scenes of snow-covered hills and hills with flowers in full bloom, radiant autumn leaves, and summer brilliance.

Chapter 13
Joy & Jubilee of the Lord

Heaven placed me on an elevator during my prayer time on December 22nd, 2021. Someone asked me if I was going up or down. I said the word "up," and the elevator went straight up through the clouds into the throne room of Heaven. Exiting the elevator, I could see many angels sounding shofars and trumpets. They were held high, and I saw them in an arc as I walked down the royal red carpet. I could see the 24 elders before the throne, laid out on their faces, worshiping God. I could see the seven lamp stands before the throne, burning with the fire of the Holy Ghost, each a different color of the seven colors of the rainbow.

The Father held up a mirror for me to see my reflection and showed me that I was weary from doing things from my soul. He instructed me to be spirit first and receive His rest. Then, an angel, whose name was Uriel, showed up with a golden scroll inside a crystal tube with a baby blue tint to it. I heard one of the elders say, "Give the scroll to the worthy one." I saw Jesus take the scroll, open it, and read. He said,

"Today I proclaim to you the joy of the Lord, the celebration of the Lord, the Jubilee of the hearts of the sons and daughters. There is a new season rising. It's rising from deep within the sons of God. It's rising inside the places that are supposed to expect and have expectancy but have grown cold of waiting."

I then saw a vision of what looked like a house blanketed with fresh snow. The sky was lit from the sun behind white clouds as it was still snowing. I peered into the house, taking notice of a boy and a girl before a fireplace celebrating the holiday on Earth known as Christmas. This was Christmas morning. I could see the excitement and joy in their faces as they were unwrapping presents and the excitement and joy in their parent's faces as they eagerly watched, rejoicing in the jubilation of their children.

I asked the Lord, what is the scene? He said, "This is the type of excitement and expectancy I am referring to. The type that is returning to the hearts of the children of God. In past seasons, the love upon the earth has grown cold, and the love in the body has grown cold. The brotherly love in keeping the commandment of loving your neighbor as yourself has waxed cold in the lives of many. This new rising season will be one of rejoicing; it will be a rebirth of the expectancy, the joy, and the jubilee that the Father wants His children to live in. He wants to give them the delights of their hearts, to delight in the ability to connect with Him. He wants them to be able to access Heaven and translate the things being released in Heaven to the earth. To do that, their hearts must be open to receiving the revelation of the joy of the Lord and the jubilee of the Lord."

"Is your heart open, boy?" the Father asked me. As I said yes, I could see myself opening up my chest. My heart appeared as if one would open two cabinet doors. I could see my heart open, and as it was the Father who put His hand upon it. I could see the rays of His ferocious love, heating darkened places, reigniting places that had grown cold, and imparting upon me the joy and jubilee of the Lord. I said by faith, I receive the joy and jubilee of the Lord into my realms. I spoke out a commissioning for my angels. I commissioned my angels to help me receive the joy and jubilee of the Lord, to steward it, and pour it out upon the lives of my family members, friends, and neighbors so that I truly love them as I love myself as commanded by the Lord God Almighty in Jesus name. The Father thanked me for coming and said there was so much more he wanted to give me. He said to stay poised with an expectancy to receive from Heaven.

On another occasion, the Holy Spirit gave me Psalm 95:1-2 to explore. As I focused on what was before me, I saw a ballroom full of children and people singing and dancing. They were shouting for joy and praising the name of the Lord. It was full of powerful worship, some on their knees crying, some on their faces, some marching around clapping and shouting. It was complete, unhindered, unrelenting, and unrestricted worship, as led by the joy of the Lord. Gregory, a man in white, introduced himself and began to instruct me on the joy of the Lord.

Gregory began, "The joy of the Lord is not just an emotion or something you pray for. It is a being, it is Jesus, it is Holy Spirit, it is Heaven's flow of limitless joy, akin to the feeling you felt when you first held your son or your daughters. The limitless *floating on cloud nine* type of joy, a feeling you hoped would last forever. These are components and characteristics of Father's love and heart. The joy of the Lord is strength to those who rest in it; revival to those who bathe in it; and a wellspring to those who drink of the deep, deep wells of Father's joy."

As he spoke these words, a rainbow-colored waterfall appeared above me and flowed down upon me. The frequency of the water falling was electrified. As it fell upon me, I could feel it vibrating through every part of my being, in every realm, through my mind, heart, soul, body, and spirit. There is a rejoicing and a springing up of joy in this season.

This morning, I was reminded of my prayer for dead things to be brought back to life. I was shown that this is an objective of joy, to bring dead things back to life, because there is joy in that. I could see a vision of Jesus, but He was on a movie screen. He was walking up to what looked like a stone structure, like a mausoleum of his day. I could see Him calling out to Lazarus, and I saw Lazarus walking out of his grave, pulling a white wrap off his face and body as he walked out. The physical manifestation of the joy of the Lord on his sisters and all who were there to see him raised back to life was visible to me. I could see the excitement, the weeping, the pure love, the heightened expression of gratitude, and praise to the Father. These were all indications of the work of the joy of the Lord in this scripture.

Jesus appeared, walking through the vision I was seeing, and put His hand upon my head. He said, "My son, I am now imbuing you with this joy and instruct that you would release it to others." Heaven's instruction to me was, "Refresh, refill, release." I could see my angels celebrating as this was happening, and as quickly as the encounter began, it was over.

Chapter 14
Place of the Miraculous

I was given a key when I asked what Heaven had for me on February 5th, 2021. I was told it's the key to the Door of Destiny. Without hesitation, I unlocked it and pushed it open. I heard, "This is a place of peace, joy, and overflow."

I then saw purple and blue clouds, a yellow radiant sun, and blue illuminated water flowing towards me. As my eyes focused more to see into the sun, I could see Jesus walking on the water toward me. The clouds were shifting colors to that of the spectrum of the rainbow. On the horizon were many angels; they were healing & ministering angels.

Jesus took me by the hand to walk back on the water with Him. He told me, "This is the place of the miraculous." The angels are assigned from here to partner with the saints. They are sent out to carry out the assignments of the miraculous based on the measure of faith exerted in prayer for others on the earth. They help aid in the signs, wonders, and miracles the Father wants to release.

There was a thick presence in this place; it is also a place of refreshing. Your spirit can access this place when ministering to others; it allows the angels to help in those areas and miracles will occur.

Words are Weapons.

While in prayer at another time, Robert, a man in white linen appeared and said, "There is a shift coming. There will be many changes; roll with the punches and allow the joy of the Lord to be your strength. Everyone in your job is experiencing this, so continue to do what you are doing, for you know how to press into the Father for your refreshing. You are to continue praying and assigning angels to patrol the community."

The sheep destined to be there are being given into your hand. Not all you see will come in, but as you co-shepherd the flock those who have it in the scroll of their destiny will be there. No matter what your earnings are in your secular job, the Father will provide. The Father's provision for you is immovable.

Suddenly two other men in white appeared, William and Malcolm. William said, "The sword or weapon of your words is mighty for the tearing down of strongholds." Malcom added "We are referring to prayer, of course. It's not just about speaking blessings or curses. The spoken word affects the unlocking of the fullness of your destiny, as well as the unlocking of those who are bound. The sound waves [of your words] have power. As the Holy Spirit thunders through your voice, unseen realities will manifest within the earth. This is faith. This is how it can be used for creation and breakthrough. (Hebrews 11) Pray bold and powerful prayers, prophecy, and profess the promises of God into your life, and you will see the abundant harvest of the wheat and new wine quickly poured into your realms. Speak it forth!! Be free and unhindered in what you're saying. Know that the Lord wishes for you to do this for His children so they can be restored to their destiny and inheritances." As this encounter concluded, I opened my Bible and began to meditate upon the scripture of reference, Hebrews 11.

Portals of Lies

I started another engagement with Jesus, where I was on a fun slide at a carnival. When I flew off, I landed in the sand on an island. Three portals opened, and these wormlike things appeared, like the worms from the Beetlejuice movie. The Lord explained that these are the enemy's lies that threaten faith, hope, and belief. He showed me how these worms could infest my thought life and get my mind going on soulish emotions; then, while my guard is down the enemy fires a dart at my heart. I saw what looked like a rock flung at a piece of glass; it starts as a small chip or crack and spreads until it is large and can break. The Lord zoomed out from the glass, and I saw that this was my heart we were looking at now from a distance. Next, he showed me my stature when my heart and thought life is under attack, slumped over, looking like the world's weight is on me. He explained this diverts me from my purpose. Then, he showed me a picture of myself standing in authority as a son with a crown, white garments, and my hand out with a determined content look like a traffic cop, halting traffic. I was stopping the plans of the adversary by standing united in Christ.

He said:

Be at peace, child; your stillness and rest in My presence is your greatest weapon against the enemy. Allow yourself time to be refreshed not just in the word but by soaking in the presence of God.

Chapter 15
River of Grace

As I stepped into Heaven on May 2nd, 2022, I saw myself in a boat on a river. The river was very calm and still. I heard the Holy Spirit telling me this is the river of grace above me. It looked like I was staring at a beautiful starry night sky where I could see the Milky Way galaxy overhead. As my eyes focused around me, I saw Jesus was in the boat with me. We approached a place resembling an edge or a waterfall, and the boat went over. However, once we went over the edge, we were still right side up; there was no fall. The boat was still coasting on this river. I heard Heaven say that they were showing me the folding of time, the awareness of the quantum realm.

A multi-dimensional capacity in different planes of existence is now being released into the earth. These concepts are challenging to wrap the human mind around, but they are foundational constructs of creation for when the Father created all you see. He made all that you do not see, all the Heavenly gates, all the realms, all the Heavens, and all the places you've traveled both in the body and the spirit.

This river of grace is peace, calming to the soul, that your spirit can guide you in knowing these things are true without fright, without questioning. Just having the grace to receive more of the revelation Father seeks to give.

The boat made a left turn, and then the nose of the boat steered straight in the direction that had been up but became forward as I was still right-side up in the boat. I heard Heaven say there is so much more to our dimensional reality than what we know or have been taught. I heard the word *gates* and got the impression that the Father was speaking of heavenly gates. They are a transit method for the angels and also a method where Heaven can imbue its power, treasures, mandates, and assignments into different facets of the earth.

Hearing this in the spirit, I could see what looked like my living room. Looking from above, I could see myself sitting on a couch, trying to receive from the Lord. Three portals were opening, and three angels came into the room out of thin air. I was shown that this was a method of travel for our angels. I instantly knew that when I call my angels near, commission them to a task, or request to talk to them, this method of travel is how they get from one place to another. If our angels are somewhere else, they can tune into our frequency and use these portals or "gates" to exit and enter our dimensional reality at that exact point. I also became aware that when a request is made for them to "come near," they use this same means of travel and transportation. Humans also can utilize these portals when walking fully immersed in the Spirit of God. This is part of the revelation of what the Father has for His sons and is restoring in this season. We can access these gates by faith.

This revelation resonated with me, and I became keenly aware that this is a heavenly technology, one by which bi-location and teleportation are possible, as evidenced in the Bible. In looking to the Word, we see Philip transporting after baptizing the man from Ethiopia (Acts 8:39), Elijah tapped into this revelation when escaping from Ahab to Jezreel (1 Kings 18:46), and even Jesus himself at the mount of Transfiguration (Matthew 17, Mark 9, Luke 9) entered such a portal with the disciples to encounter Heaven.

As the visual part of this encounter resumed, the boat suddenly stopped. I saw a dock, and Jesus helped me out of the boat. He put one hand on my heart and one hand on my head and said, "My child, I bless you to receive this revelation with ease, to grow in it, to teach it, to steward it, and to use it for the Father's glory, amen." I said, "Amen," in agreement with him, and was back in the natural, in awe of what I had just come to understand.

Expanding The River of God

At another time, I saw many boats with people on them, and I heard they were river rafting on the river of God. I heard the Lord say he was expanding the river of God in me this season to provide further knowledge and wisdom. When you flow freely on God's river, you will have peace and ease to coast through life. Worry and fear will not overcome you, be provoked to press into Father for this river issues forth from His throne and is an inheritance for all His sons. It is for His Bride and those who seek Him with an undivided heart. Incline your ear to the softness and stillness of His voice, and the hidden mysteries of the Kingdom will unfold to you.

Wellspring of Refreshing

In another encounter, I stepped into Heaven and saw a tall staircase made of water. The water steps were each radiating a different color from the rainbow. As I reached the top step, I saw a vast fountain; I heard Holy Spirit say, "This is the wellspring of life, the wellspring of refreshing." This fountain had many different spigots shooting living water in the air in rhythm with the music and cadences of Heaven. I heard the Lord's voice giving me instructions; in the natural, I was glancing over news headlines of 2 shootings that happened that weekend.

Jesus said, "You will see an uptick in the violence and hardships even past what you're witnessing. As you move toward the turn of the year, it will escalate and become even more unstable and concerning than things appear now." He continued, "Do not lose hope, for alas, all who call on My name will be saved. Tribulation and judgment are indeed coming upon the lawless and unjust, but awakening and revival are also coming. Revival is coming to stir up a reinvigoration of those called by My name. They are to embrace the fullness of what I've called them to and raise a new front-line generation of those redeemed from death and the grave to be set upon a path of eternal life."

The Father's voice broke in, and He said:

Walk in the Heavens daily, My son. It is in this realm that you have access to, which will refresh you and fill you up to be able to walk amidst the chaos with a joy-filled, tender, and compassionate heart. Although the days seem increasingly evil when you are solely focused on My throne, you will taste and see these days are increasingly good.

My child, do not let the delusions and busyness of the world derail you. Come and drink from the well of My refreshing presence, by which you will be fed, refreshed, and rejuvenated. Your path is riddled with twists, turns, and wonderous surprises. The tension caused by mundane and rote actions of tradition will cause you to feel dry and irritable. Seek me and all I have to offer that you may pour out and into others and be refueled for the journey. All you set your intention to accomplish will be carried out when you are walking under the shadow of My wing. Hide yourself in Me when you're feeling weak, and I will give you the rest that soothes and satisfies.

In another encounter, the Father walked me up to a well. It was called the Wellspring of Refreshing. I screamed down into it and heard my voice echo. He lowered down a bucket and pulled it up, filled with living water. He instructed me not to shortcut time spent in the valley (low places that felt empty). Father said, "This valley was a time of building relationship with Him in the low place; the "to" in going from glory to glory." He further instructed me by saying, "Don't shortcut this time; it is precious."

He continued,

Child, there have been things you were taught that were wrong. Things you believed that were amiss. This is a time of refining and redefining. Serve admirably in the pain and the place of woundedness. You will experience the most profound growth and expansion, like a flower that blossoms from a barren and pruned branch.

I then prayed and asked Father to prune the dead branches and leaves off me so I can bear the fruit of love, which gives birth to joy that births peace, patience, kindness, and self-control.

Suddenly, I saw an entity that my spirit understood was the frequency of love. It manifested as living musical notes and musical scales. It appeared like sheet music, except the notes were alive and flew off the page, wrapping around me. The notes were pink in color. The musical staff also came alive and wrapped around me like bandages wrapped around a mummy. Collectively, they went into my heart, and my body started vibrating at the frequency of love in Heaven. I could feel as if my body was buzzing, and in the vision, I saw waves come out in many colors—first blue, then yellow, then green, then red.

I understood this was a living entity; it was the power of love. It could be released from our hearts to others as the Father released His love to us. As I prayed, and, by faith, released the frequency of love, I could feel a shift and the movement of the Holy Spirit throughout my body.

I bless you to receive the frequency of love into your realms as you read this. May your realms be overtaken by the overarching love of the Father. May you radiate His unfailing love to all you encounter.

Wellspring of Life

In another encounter, I saw four angels playing in a fountain. I asked what it was and was told it was the wellspring of life pouring forth from the fountain of refreshing; I climbed in and just began to float in the water. Jesus was there with me, and He just smiled and marveled at me with eyes filled with immense love and adoration. He said,

> *My dear boy, you are so loved, blessed beyond measure, fearfully and wonderfully made, and destined for greatness. Do not let the frequencies of the realm you occupy shift your focus from having a Kingdom mentality. Let your mindset overflow with the peace of God and Kingdom realities. All things upon the earth are not as they seem, but in Heaven, they are transparent and can be received at face value.*
>
> *Do not let your heart and emotions be hindered and locked up from your surroundings but remain unbound and forever outpouring the Father's love that flows freely from the firmament through your being and out through your belly. This is the river that proceeds forth from the Father's throne. Allow yourself to be poised to receive that which is long desired to be poured out to you. This season is one of*

exponential growth; to grow, you must go through tests, trials, and opportunities for development. Correction is never fun, but it helps to bear good fruit.

As I looked past Him, I could see we were in a garden with tall trees in the distance with all kinds of fruit on them—good fruit. I started professing my love and said, "Use me as you see fit, God. Trim every branch that doesn't bear fruit, remove everything that doesn't serve you. Equip me with a heart of compassion and empathy for the needs of others. Help me to know your heart more."

Immediately, He picked me up out of the water, and we were soaring through the clouds on the back of a giant eagle. Jesus said, "You are called to be a prophet to the nation." I saw a boat house with a ravine beside it and empty boats floating in the water. I asked what the boats were for.

The Lord told me they symbolize those not yet floating on the rivers of living water. It was time for the harvest; the boats would be filled, the vessels filled with His spirit. The time of awakening is now; the time of revival is at hand. It will not look like anything that has come before, and nothing after will be like this one. In modern Earth time, when most think of revival, they expect it to look like Azusa Street, tent revivals of the 50's or the 70's, and the Jesus people movement, but what is coming is unfathomable to the confines of the human mind. The Father's thoughts are bigger, and His purposes are unsearchable. This next move will be built on the backs of those who were unwilling to follow Jesus unreservedly. Those called will be as those He first called; the ones society had cast out will be first in line to receive His Kingdom and greater glory.

In the spirit, three men in white were near me: A.A. Allen, Oral Roberts, and Smith Wigglesworth. Behind them, a multitude of saints, revivalists, prophets, and men and women of God. The Lord said,

I have a place for you in this; I have a place prepared for you, My child.

As He spoke, I could see the prayer and impartation of the saints like lightning shooting through the crowd. The lightning struck my chest; I could feel the revivalist mantle had been traded into me and landed on me. As the Lord put His hand on my head, I could feel an activation of the healing virtue flow within me.

I heard the Holy Spirit say,

Not just a prophet, more than a prophet, a revivalist.

A day of rising will be coming, you're being refined and prepared. Your weakness is made perfect by My strength, trust in me.

I could see the angels and saints dancing and celebrating, then the ground disappeared. There was a swirling portal above and souls going up to Heaven. I also saw a portal swirling below and souls going down to the abyss. In between was the galactic plane. I heard, "The wheat is being sifted into the storehouses."

Chapter 16
Encounter with the Spirit of Faith

As I was reading the Word on June 8th, 2022, I started seeing in the spirit and beheld a small blue and white fire. This flame could speak, and while its edges were electric blue, the inside was bright white. It was the spirit of faith, God's faith. Its voice sounded feminine and it introduced itself saying, "I am faith." I noted the stature of faith and its size and said, "Wow, you're so small." Faith interrupted me and said, "Correct, like the size of a mustard seed," which reminded me of the Matthew 13 parable of the mustard seed.

I was ministered to in my spirit by the spirit of Faith with Hebrews 11:1 and 2 Corinthians 4:13-14 about faith and its role. Faith spoke to me and said, "Now, child, I work in the hearts of the believers to steward the gift of faith. I work In the hearts of those who are fertile soil, ready to move forward in faith. I work with them to believe for the many things God has placed before them to access by faith, with complete trust in the Father. I help them to have unwavering trust and determination to operate as sons, knowing that all is created by Him and provided by Him who is at work in His sons through His Holy Spirit."

I instantly knew that the gift of faith is precious and necessary for accessing Heaven and bringing eternal realities into the earth. I was then shown a vision in the spirit. I saw myself praying for others on a prayer line at the food pantry I once volunteered at. This was a vision of this activity from a Heavenly vantage point.

I heard Faith say, "Look hard in the spirit." Looking intently, I could see the power of prayer at work. I could see the words of my faith as daggers coming out of my mouth in frequencies of silver and gold. The words struck down imps and demons seated on the shoulders and backs of the people being prayed over. As the forces of darkness were pushed back, I could see angels swooping in and decimating, capturing, and dismantling strongholds. I saw them battling in territories within generations that the enemy had illegally claimed a stake in.

Suddenly, I noticed what looked like an explosion. Golden Heavenly light came out of a Heavenly portal over the heads of those being prayed for. This was the glory of God bathing them and bringing ease to their weary souls. I saw words of knowledge as bricks falling into place. These words were building a new foundation in the lives of these individuals. Rivers of living water filled them with fresh faith and belief that God would answer these prayers.

I saw myself in the days afterward, walking through moments when the opposition seemed intense. Then, I had a vision of days following these events that led to hearing the breakthroughs that came from those prayers. I received a revelation that as sons of God, there will be times when we will know God answered a prayer by faith. We may never hear a follow-up or a testimony. Other times, there will be a stirring up of our faith when we hear how God answered and miraculously handled the situations we had prayed for.

I heard Faith say,

You are a daring child of God, one who is unafraid to ask for all things in proportion to your faith even if you aren't sure it is Father's will. You still don't hesitate to ask. This is the proving ground of your faith. It will bring new levels of boldness and new levels of freedom.

Travail until you prevail, battle until you see a breakthrough, and press in when you are pressed down. The Father's faith is limitless. Don't hesitate to call on it when you're feeling empty. He is just, righteous, and faithful to lift you and send you out.

With that, the flame of faith entered my heart, and our encounter ended.

Gift of Faith

At another time, I walked across a golden archway into a field. The field had the most beautiful, deep green grass I had seen. There were white picket fences, the purest white, and many children were running around playing. Jesus was seated on the ground, in the center, marveling. A portal opened as I walked towards him, and Abraham and Job walked through to greet me with Enoch. Jesus motioned for me to sit down beside Him. As I did, He put His arm around my shoulder. The others sat down as well, facing me. Heaven said:

> *Look upon all of these; they are the seeds of promise. These are those more numerous than the grains of sand on the seashore, more radiant than all the stars in the sky. These are the promise of the generations, the past, the present, and the future in the realm of time. Only to continue to exist through the expansion and collaboration of the generations, the other side, those that Abraham waited and waited to see the fullness and the manifestation of the words. What the Father had spoken came to fruition in His life. These are those which Job had received after losing all he had been blessed with. The promise of hope, the seed of love, and the expansion of faith; these are those who have carried the message of Enoch walking so closely with the Father that he could step*

out of the realm of time and into eternity at will, ultimately choosing to dwell here in eternity.

Jesus said,

My beloved child, your times, seasons, and steps are ordered. Not one word of what your Father has promised you shall fall to the ground.

As Jesus said this, three of the children had walked over. They were mine, yet to be born. All three came and sat down on my lap. I wrapped my arms around them and hugged them all at once. Jesus said,

Your spirit recognizes the fullness in the manifestation of what already exists and what has yet to be birthed. Your soul is where the inconsistencies lie, My child.

Allow the winds of revelation to stir the waters of your soul; to be still, and to receive, to know that it is done. It is already set in motion; the moment you chose complete obedience to step out by faith and get back on course is when your prayers were answered. There is no need to be downcast or worrisome. There is no need to grow weary in your waiting; be cheerful and full of joy, and know that, although this is a promise you desire in your heart, My greatest joy is seeing your face delight in the fulfillment of My promises.

Oh child, how My heart swells with love when My children see their faith and their expectation met with an answer to prayer, with the manifestation of things contended for, and the increase of hope. It is not My will for My children to be kept waiting, or to lose faith and embrace doubt. Those are lies of the earth, but here in Heaven, as you believe a thing, think a thing, or set your intention toward a thing, instantly it manifests!

Look at the parable of the fig tree. As I commanded it to shrivel and bear no more fruit, instantly it did so.

Your faith is instantaneous; the gift of faith you have been given is a gift of instantaneous faith, My son. Not only shall you see fast answers to prayer for others that you intercede for, but in your own life, you will start to see more of a rapid response as you pray. As you come to me with full expectation and trust, you will know this is because you obeyed me. Your heart is turned towards me, your intentions are pure, and you are being called to minister to a generation.

Jeremy, Jeremiah, My beloved son, what you have seen thus far, even the increase from just a few weeks ago, is nothing compared to what you will experience by the end of this month. Let your expectations and faith be raised, elevated, and expecting God's goodness in an incomprehensible and unfathomable measure.

As Jesus spoke, I wept, knowing He knows our hearts. He sees our deepest desires and innermost thoughts and truly cares for each of us.

It is a fearful thing to fall into the hands of the living God. (Hebrews 10:31) (NKJV)

Chapter 17
Encounter with the Citizens of Heaven

I stepped into Heaven one January morning and saw many babies in the spirit dressed in suits, standing with the Lord. They stood upright as men but were in the form of children. I heard the Lord speak. He said,

> *These are the ones whose destinies had been aborted on the earth, whose lives were stolen, who were deprived of breathing the breaths I set forth for them and enjoying the life I had intended for them. These are the ones who have been killed and destroyed for My name's sake. Who have been persecuted and murdered horrifically; these are the ones My heart has been broken for, and those who are being redeemed as the seal is broken and My elect are being saved. They still have an eternal destiny to live out in My Kingdom. The men of the earth had hated and slaughtered them, but we (Father, Son, and Holy Spirit) have loved them and have hurt for the injustices done to them.*

As I heard these words, I saw a multitude of people before the throne; a large angel handed Jesus a scroll. He opened it and read aloud,

> *Judgment has come to all mankind, the righteous and unrighteous, the wicked and good, the saved and lost, the backslidden and downtrodden. Who will hear the wail of the Lord and the Father's broken heart? Which of you will repent for the injustices that have tipped the scales of Heaven? Who will incline their ear and know that it is the Father's pleasure to give the Kingdom to His sons who are deserving of such a precious gift?*

As Jesus spoke in the middle of the room, I could see the whole Earth and many people on it. Only a few stepped forward to stand in the gap and repent. I could see that I had not been one of them. I fell on my face in the spirit and said,

> *Father, I repent for not being one who had stood in the gap as an intercessor and a watchman. Please forgive me for a wayward heart; forgive me for idly standing by and not seeking you with My whole heart on these matters.*

As I repented, Jesus wept. He grabbed my shoulder and stood me up; I could see I was transformed. The dust of this day was washed away. I stood holding a child, and when I put that child down, I saw many children standing behind him. I led a charge before them, holding a shield and a sword in my hand, the Word of God. I asked what the meaning was and heard God say, "These are the ones whose lives and generations will be saved for the work I have called you to in this very hour." As I charged forward, ahead of these little ones, I saw a ring of white light pressing forward, emanating outward into the darkness and lighting up the night before me. The night became day, and I heard these were the angels of the Lord being sent before us on this path to wage war against that which opposed the assignment the Father had set for these seasons.

Then I saw myself frail and elderly in a wheelchair, my wife by my side. I knew this moment in my timeline was near the end of my time in this realm. Many people surrounded us. They were honoring us and telling us about things we had done, some which we had long forgotten, some which we had never previously seen an impact, nor desired to know the outcome. They told us how we had blessed them and how we had saved their lives, how we had shown them there is a God, and how they had been taught of His love for them through us.

Suddenly, I was sitting on the shoreline in eternity, gazing off into eternity's oceans. Jesus put His arm around me and said, "With you, My son, I am well pleased!"

This is a season where I will strip you bare, naked, and make you anew. The old-world knowledge will be burnt out of your very existence, and the hindrances to My Spirit's flow in your life will be gone entirely. You will learn the art of patience; I ask that you lean into it. Let me speak to you in this secret place. I have brought you here for rest, but I have also brought you here to be refined.

Be not as one who is angered in laborless moments; be not one who is embittered by seasons that seem lengthy, but be a son at peace. The peace of God shall flow like a river, in you and through you, and though sudden destruction will come like a thief in the night, you and your tribe, your disciples shall be delivered from it. The season is now. Will your heart burn with passion for me? Or will you allow laziness to camp in your heart where the fire would burn for me?

An Encounter with the Cloud of Witnesses

In worship on the morning of September 19th, 2021, I was transported to Heaven and was on my face before the throne of the Lord. I was crying, repenting, and heavy-hearted from being distant from the Father's loving embrace. The Father grabbed me and held me with a loving embrace. As worship continued in the natural and the spirit of holiness descended upon the church, I was on my face crying out to the Lord. I saw angels pulling out of me that which didn't belong. Holy

Spirit told me that they were smiting forces of darkness that had come against me.

Suddenly, I saw a bunch of men in white linen coming up; first was my brother in Heaven, Dana Robin. He traded into me favor, a blessing of the firstborn. He explained that since he was not born in the natural and was first, I was robbed of this, and this would manifest favor. Then I saw Job, who traded into me the covenant with eyes and faithfulness to the wife given by God. Next, I saw Isaiah and Jeremiah. Jeremiah traded into me the weeping and crying of the Lord through intercession and Isaiah the prophetic gifting of reading and proclaiming the Word of the Lord. Then I saw Samuel, who gave me a staff and a horn of oil; he traded into me the discernment of being a kingmaker and knowing how to use that call appropriately as a prophet. After Samuel, I saw King David, who traded into me the heart of worship and the heart of being focused on the Lord, forsaking the world. The clean heart and understanding of intimacy in worship. Next, Moses traded into me leadership. Finally, Abraham the knowledge of being a friend of God.

> *You're my place of quiet retreat, and your wraparound presence becomes My shield as I wrap myself in your Word! (Psalms 119:114) (TPT)*

I heard,

Seek greater intimacy with the Lord, only His presence will truly comfort you and restore you to what you have been called to move in!

Here I am, doing a new thing; Now it is springing up— do you not know about it? I will surely make a way in the desert, rivers in the wasteland. (Isaiah 43:19)

...be renewed in the spirit of your mind and put on the new self—created to be like God in true righteousness and holiness. So, lay aside lying and 'each one of you speak truth with His neighbor,' for we are members of one another. 'Be angry, yet do not sin.' Do not let the sun go down on your anger, nor give the devil a foothold. The one who steals must steal no longer—instead he must work, doing something useful with his own hands, so he may have something to share with the one who has need. Let no harmful word come out of your mouth, but only what is beneficial for building others up according to the need, so that it gives grace to those who hear it. Do not grieve the Ruach ha-Kodesh of God, by whom you were sealed for the day of redemption. Get rid of all bitterness and rage and anger and quarreling and slander, along with all malice. Instead, be kind to one another,

compassionate, forgiving each other just as God in Messiah also forgave you. (Ephesians 4:23-32) (TLV)

The Celestial Cloud of Witnesses

As I stepped into Heaven on January 6th, 2023, I called my angels near and started to engage Heaven and my personal star for my daily scroll. When I took my position of rest to govern, I could see Jesus in the Bright and Morning star. I also saw what looked like heavenly blue lightening zipping between all the stars. It was His power working through us, it electrified the star which started to glow in a multitude of colors and shockwaves of blue and white light. This light emanated outward from its core in a ring-shaped pattern connecting with the cosmos around me and touching my business stars, family's stars and the Heavens. I suddenly had a knowing of the presence of the cosmic cloud of witnesses. These beings appear as a group of individuals in light bodies, the way they speak and interact I can only explain as being a frequency that is understandable by the Spirit of God within me. The sound made when they speak is much like the sound of ice crushing against ice, electrical currents, and a string wind blowing. As they speak, light emanates from where their mouths are, they speak in one accord, in complete unity.

I heard Heaven explain,

These are the hosts of Heaven, ancient ones, who bear witness to all creation. The delivering work of the sons of the most high God who have set out to sit enthroned in sonship and reconquer the cosmos should become acquainted with them. With their help cosmic revelation shall be revealed.

Again, I heard:

They are the hosts of Heaven, ancient ones, who bear witness to all creation being built and established.

I noted this must be important as it was repeated in more detail. "Their designed function is to trade into galaxies, planets, entire civilizations, the riches, minerals, revelation, and elements. (These appeared as a substance that was like nutrients and particles.) The universe is alive, the realms are living entities, and all creation is living and breathing, crying out for the Glory of the Lord. All that has been created plays a part in the grand symphony created by the orchestra of God, Yahweh, the creator." As I heard these things, I could see how they view the Father; the imagery was both awesome and terrifying. I was only given a glimpse of this once but was familiar with this as I had beheld His greatness in this form one time before. The fear of the Lord overcame me at one look of this incredible and terrifying figure. I was completely awestruck.

I could see what was referred to as the grand symphony. This referred to the power of frequency and sound waves. All creation makes sound; the stars and planets have sounds they use to praise the Lord. The rocks literally cry out, plants and trees, waters, animals and people, even the tiniest of insects. All were intricately designed and interwoven to "play their instruments" and praise almighty God, all creation sings.

The Beings of Many Waters

In another engagement, I had seen four swirls of water, almost like water tornados. As they touched the ground, they started forming in the figure of a being. They remained translucent but resembled a human figure. I was told these were beings of the cosmic cloud of witnesses, not unlike the men in white and classes of angels that operate in the Heavenlies. They are living waters, their voices like many waters. From them flows the river of life, healing, joy, and refreshing. As I understood with My spirit, they were crying HOLY unto the Lord, their voices lifted up and sounded like the babbling of a brook, the trickling of a stream, the crashing of waves, and the pounding of a waterfall pouring onto rocks. They were both soft and thunderous, sounding all at once.

Chapter 18
Encounter with the Goodness of God

The next encounter was a reminder of Romans 2:4 and how the goodness of God leads us to repentance. This occurred on July 3rd, 2022, and was a few days after I had moved my family to Florida from New York.

I had an encounter with a man at a local Waffle House. The Lord nudged me to speak to and pray for him. When I was obedient, I could feel the presence of Heaven upon our lives as I prayed and ministered to him. As I finished praying, he began to confess his sins (as this man had a religious background.) I felt the Lord instructing me to minister my testimony and told him Jesus paid sins' debt; we only need to repent directly to the Father in Heaven. He rededicated his life to Jesus that instant, and we prayed for him to be spirit-filled and spirit-led.

I was taken aback by how God showed up when I was obedient to pray for this stranger and moved by how the goodness of God led him to repentance.

Later that day in a Target, I had difficulty with our oldest child being bitter, resentful, and angry about the move. He wanted a volleyball net, but I wasn't willing to reward a bad attitude. We went to the sports aisle, and he saw a football he liked and a volleyball set. I put the football and the volleyball set he wanted in the shopping cart as I chose grace and mercy over anger; he was surprised. I told him that if he acted correctly and politely and gave things a chance, I would do whatever he wanted. I said, "You need to apologize," and he went to his mom and apologized for his attitude with a repentant heart.

The Father showed me His goodness will do likewise for us and bring us to repentance.

Or do you belittle the riches of His kindness and tolerance and patience—not realizing that God's kindness leads you to repentance? (Romans 2:4) (TLV)

Tongues of Fire

One morning, as I often do, I entered the heavenly realms in the spirit. We do this legally and correctly through Jesus, who is the door (John 10:9). As I stepped in, it was like going through a wormhole. I could see stars and then was surrounded by light. I was standing on limestone or sandstone on a very high wall. When I looked down below, I saw trees, then I jumped off the wall and floated down to the ground. Looking up, I saw the trees were very tall.

There were deer nearby, drinking from a pond with many trees and mountains in the distance. I saw a stream and fish jumping in it. Then I saw my angel with some other angels; these were angels that I was not yet acquainted with. One was a fiery angel named Aerial; he gave me a tongue of fire and told me to eat it so that I would speak the Word of God with fire. Then he gave me another multicolored tongue to be put in my heart, and the fire would consume me because God is a consuming fire; His mantle of fire was upon me. I saw a meadow and some brown horses; I could hear the wind, streams, and waterfalls. There was a treasure chest in front of me. I opened it, and there were some scrolls. They were the expanded scrolls of my destiny, side missions, and extensions of my destiny and assignments.

Tongues

In another engagement, the Holy Spirit gave me a lesson on this precious gift. He said,

The interpretation of tongues is not a cheap parlor trick but is for the building up of churches and individuals in the body. Much of the Father's knowledge can be released through tongues. Heavenly planes are navigated by angelic beings, and

portals of worship are re-opened because strongholds are torn down by the use of this precious gift. The speaking in tongues stirs up the believer's spirit and will unlock the realms of Heavenly revelation. The Father wishes to impart upon you. Use it frequently and pray fervently and constantly!

Wheat and Tares

One summer morning, I entered the business complex of Heaven, and upon asking for my daily agenda, I was told to go into the biome for a meeting. The biome appeared to be an agricultural area that resembled what a farm in the countryside may look like. I ventured into the wheat fields to meet with the Father and the Lord Jesus. When I arrived, they greeted me, and the Lord began explaining the parable of the wheat and tares. He said that I am like the wheat; the tares represent those in the world, not bearing fruit or at the current time are of no Heavenly use. The wheat represents those whose eyes are fixed on the Kingdom of Heaven and engaging the Father and His Kingdom. It is not the Father's will that any of the world should be included, the tares or lost, but that all should be wheat, that we would be gathered into vats and used for His purposes.

Jesus explained that I am like wheat, and if I look up the process by which wheat is harvested and refined to make bread and cakes, I would understand the process I am currently going through, where I feel beaten and pressed. That is what I was experiencing. I am being refined and transformed to be who the Father wants me to become.

I was encouraged to be firm in my faith, and He told me that I am the beloved of God and that they (God, Jesus, Holy Spirit) are proud. I am doing a fine job.

Chapter 19

The Armies of Heaven

I found myself standing on what appeared to be an aircraft carrier, moving across the sea. I heard the spirit of the Lord say, "This aircraft carrier is not the type one would see upon the earth." I noticed no warplanes as I looked around the ship's deck. I saw angels in battle stations, armed and ready to be dispatched. The Lord said, "These are the ones being sent out upon the earth to fight on behalf of My children." He revealed that He was about to move swiftly upon the earth for His sons' and daughters' lives, marriages, and children's lives. He reminded me despite the pains of current circumstances experienced in the natural realm, weeping only lasts for a night, but joy comes in the morning.

Jesus spoke again, saying, "Angels are being sent down to destroy the plans and tactics of the forces that seek to destroy hope and joy in the hearts of the sons of God. The enemy has come to kill, steal, and destroy hopes and dreams, but I have come to deliver the righteous." The Lord and His righteous armies are fighting an all-out war against the forces of darkness. This is done to bring all His promises to pass for the good of those He loves, His sons and His daughters.

Bilocation & Pocket Realms

In another angelic encounter, I found myself entering the business complex of Heaven. Immediately, I was taken to a place called *The Salon* to refresh my spirit. After standing under a shower of the living waters, I was told to go to the seventh floor of the business complex. Upon reaching the elevator, I noticed that it was a glass enclosure where you could see out over the whole business complex as you're in the elevator. I went up to the seventh floor and noticed a big empty office space, but in the center of it was something that looked like a transport portal that one could stand on. My personal angel, Philip, explained that this could transport me anywhere in the heavenly realm. As I looked out of the windows, I noticed such places as the healing gardens, the court complex, the Father's house, and other various areas from different vantage points in the office space on the seventh floor. After speaking to my angel, I stepped onto the portal and was instantly transported to an old place, a cabin in the woods. Inside this cabin is what I call a *glory shower*. When you stand under it, you can feel the radiance of the Father's glory pouring out upon you and refreshing you. In this instance, I was given revelation on bilocation and transportation. In the spirit, you can occupy two spaces at the same time. My spirit was still on the seventh floor, speaking with my angel Philip, and at the same time was also walking through the wilderness area and opening the door to the cabin. It was like watching a split screen on a TV, yet I was experiencing both things simultaneously. I was experiencing typing on a keyboard in the business complex, pulling up a video feed on a computer on the seventh-floor office space, and at the same time walking into the cabin and standing under the glory shower receiving from the Father. I felt His glorious love, but then my spirit was instantly back in one spot. I was shown through this how a location in the spirit works.

I was then told about pocket realms and how they can be opened up in and out of time and space as offensive and defensive strategies and protocols against the adversary.

Working in Unison

As I stepped into the business complex on another occasion, I was taken to my conference room. I could see it was expanded and upgraded. Some new faces (angels and people in white linen) were now assigned to some of the ventures I was engaging Heaven in.

I felt the need to commission all the angels to work in unison; as I had done this, I saw Abraham, Moses, and Jesus join us.

I heard Jesus speak and say, "Your authority and jurisdiction are expanding like the flocks of Kedar. This rapid growth is explosive; you will need to be more intentional about engaging Heaven to manage it, flow with Heaven's resources, and build it out."

He continued, "The foundations have been constructed, but now is the time when the pump has been primed, and Heaven's flow shall be poured out upon you (and your family in greater measure)."

Abraham handed me a cylindrical map, much like a kaleidoscope or spyglass. As I peered inside, I could see each of these establishments and the efforts of them individually. I could see myself with my sleeves rolled up, working in them, and others with me helping to build. Many would be supported through these ventures.

As I reviewed this, I could see the conference room table was like a river or stream of water that had a waterfall at one end and was filling the room with water. It never ran dry, and I heard, "The Father's resources are limitless; use and steward them well."

The Father's Excitement

One morning, my angels presented me with a burst of fireworks that did not dissipate; they stayed radiantly lit. It was like a holographic statue. I heard Heaven say, this is the

Father's excitement over you as a son. As I received this precious gift into my heart, I was told that this is symbolic of the Father's excitement over His children.

I was told to think as a child on the Fourth of July. The excitement that comes with running around in the warm summer air, barbecues, eating watermelon, and seeing the displays of beautiful, radiant fireworks exploding throughout the sky. This brought me back to when I was a child and enjoyed these things. I heard the verse in my spirit about not preventing the children from coming to Jesus and inheriting the Kingdom of God. With His excitement, awe, and wonder, we are to embrace what the Father is excited about, that which the Father marvels over each of His children. I could feel that the Spirit of the Lord inside of me wanted to burst forth with excitement.

Suddenly, I saw Jesus appear; as He walked into the scene, it was as if He was walking on the stardust. It was like He had walked on water straight through the vast darkness of the galaxy. I could see all creation bowing to Him in reverence and worship. As I joined in, my spirit cried out that *He is HOLY.* Suddenly, we were in the Throne Room of Heaven where stars had been moments ago. I could see the angels and the saints and beyond them all creation worshipping Him, crying, Holy.

Chapter 20
Exposing and Defeating Darkness

I was lying in the arms of Jesus one morning, crying out and thanking Him for all He has done. I saw a vision of octopus tentacles trying to grab me and a sword slicing off the arms and putting the entity down. Suddenly, I felt the need to commission my angels, and upon asking what they needed at that moment, Heaven had told me to request the following items:

- Thunder and lightning arrows.
- Electrified fences.
- Walls of fire, shields.
- Curtains & veils.
- Electrified harpoons and tridents.

I commissioned my angels immediately, instructing them to use these weapons to war against water and marine spirits. I could see lakes nearby in the spirit, suddenly electrified. I had a vision of the angels electrocuting and frying snakes, water dragons, python spirits, and other entities. As the angels used these tools, the entities of darkness were forced up and out of their hiding places.

Marine & Water Spirits

As I inquired as to what just had happened, The Lord spoke and told me:

These demons are dumb. Marine and water spirits are the most evil, depraved, and sinister in the kingdom of darkness. They try to move by stealth at deep levels undetected but are by far the most disgusting princes of wickedness.

The Father holds it in special regard to deal destructive blows against these enemies and takes deep pleasure in destroying their plans against His children.

For millennia, man had looked to the sea as its source of energy, food, sustenance, and trade. Man had made wishes upon bodies of water and bowed low before such abominable creatures. Man had lusted after the fantasyland that lurked deep beneath the sea and traded his seed for wealth when, in fact, it led to physical and spiritual poverty that ransacked families and generations. On this day, the Father is exposing the most wicked of all to take back all that is His and yours.

The frontline imps and minor forces had been beaten back with the revelation of bonds and through trusts, princes are now being dealt finishing blows that have made the kingdom of darkness bleed. The treasures of hell have been emptied and poured out for the sons of God to reclaim as their own in this season.

The onslaught of the marine and water kingdoms is a last-ditch effort by Lucifer to retrieve what has been lost and cash in on millennia-old vouchers pledged to darkness by ancestors who were wrongly aligned with familiar spirits and Baal.

Deeper revelation, deliverance, and prayer life are needed in this season. To forge ahead unhindered, you need to go deeper in me and with me.

I saw what looked like a golden deep-sea diver's suit in front of me. The Lord said that this was battle gear for this day and the journey ahead. There was a giant gold trident and harpoon gun with it. I was told to receive it by faith and prophetically launch these weapons in all directions at marine and water spirits aligned against me and my family.

I asked the Lord if there was anything else I needed to know, and I heard the words, "Prepare for war." As I looked up, I could see a physical manifestation and confirmation of this word in print on my bookshelf.

The Marine Kingdom

On another occasion, I requested a tutor to instruct me on the marine kingdom and how to receive deliverance from it. I saw a man in white named Marshall, who was the teacher on the subject, and he escorted me into a classroom. Jesus met us there and said He was there to observe and support me in this learning process. Marshall began by discussing some of the princes of the marine kingdom: leviathan, queen of the Atlantic, Dagon, queen of India, incubi, and succubus.

As he spoke, I could see a map of the whole earth. In every ocean on the map, I took notice of images of these entities. They were all over the waterways and seas. Some looked like dragons, others like serpents, others like merfolk, others still like squid or a Kraken. As I saw this, Marshall said, "Every myth on Earth has true origins." He could see I was uneasy at receiving all this, and he said, "Do not worry or fear; defeated foes in the sea are like every other defeated foe; they are destined for hellfire."

I took a breath. He continued, "These entities are stubborn but just as easily defeated in the courts. However, it is man's unwillingness to part with the physical pleasure of sexual sin, gratification, immorality, and greed that makes these so difficult to remove for those who keep inviting them back in. Intercessory fire built up by the fire of God on a believer's life is what will dry up their resources and see their demise is met speedily." In Matthew 17:15, the demon possessing the boy gets flung in fire, and the river is being oppressed by a water spirit from this kingdom, notice it tries to drag him off to the "river." Jesus' instruction is simple.

Jesus spoke up and said exactly what He said to His disciples in the scriptures:

...this kind goes out through prayer and fasting. (Matthew 17:21) (TLV)

Jesus said, "These entities are much more common than you think, but they try to remain hidden and believe they operate in stealth. This is why this seems so new and foreign, but much of what you have already encountered in your Christian walk and learning spiritual warfare is useful for defeating such entities."

I asked Jesus about an unwanted perverse dream I had last night and the dark entity I had seen in it. He said that it is called a siren; they are part of this kingdom and seduce mankind into evil and perverse acts through the witchcraft sent against their mind. When people's emotions are raw and unhinged, they are more susceptible to these attacks. In short, the flesh nature will lead them on a path to destruction if they are not wise to the tricks and traps of the marine kingdom.

I asked if there were specific weapons I could equip the angels with to fight such things. Marshall said, "Capture bags (for territories), tridents that spear these entities, electrified lassos, water dispeller and the tool of drought."

I asked him what the tool of *drought* is. He informed me that it is just like its name, as it dries up the resources of a marine spirit, much like a fish out of water; the fish would then die. This incredibly weakens and traps the marine spirit in order to dispose of it.

After this, I requested these for my angels and commissioned them to use these weapons.

Phantoms

In another tutorial lesson, I received instructions about dealing with phantoms. I was told phantoms operate much like how you would see the angels operate when you ask for invisibility cloaks. The difference is that the forces of darkness cannot see the angels coming when using the invisibility cloaks, but all angels can see phantoms in their activity. They operate by shrouding and cloaking activities of the enemy and other active classes of demons. By taking out the phantom it reveals the activities of the enemy. You can commission your angels to expose and round up the phantoms and everything else, working in tandem with them.

Revelation of the Evil Behind the Media

I heard Heaven say one day, "The witchcrafts of the media are trauma, torment, and fear." I saw visions of newspapers in the gas station, sitting in piles. I noticed the physical reaction of revulsion I had to the piles and also noticed there were creatures attached to them. They were spirits of trauma, torment, and fear. I saw visions of people reading the newspapers, watching the news on TV, and even on news websites on the internet. These three spirits poured off the medium like snakes. They slithered in through their eyes and ears and coiled fully around the people watching, cocooning them in a shell of demonic frequencies that agree with fear, anxiety, and worry.

I noticed my angels and Jesus there with me, as I observed things the enemy uses the news for.

Jesus spoke and said:

This is how they hatch evil schemes and have them hammered into the minds of unsuspecting victims who are tormented day and night-robbed of sleep from the horror show that is the news of the earth realm.

Later, I asked, can you show me the opposite within the walk with the Lord?

Immediately, I could see someone reading their Bible. As they ate of the word and fellowship, led with God through the word, I could see angels in the area surrounding and ministering to the believer. I could see what appeared as a gold blanket of the glory of God enveloping the scene. There was a peace that was irrevocable settling in.

Then I saw another scene where Christian worship music was playing. I could see angels dancing and twirling. People were dancing, and there was a tangible manifestation of joy.

As instruments were played, the musical notes came alive and flowed through the scene. The notes were dancing and joyous, full of the rhythm of Heaven; it was life-giving.

I saw a third scene where someone was being prayed for. The one receiving prayer had a heavy, dark, weighted blanket over them: a blanket of burden. It affected everything in their life, but as they received prayer, I could see the blanket lifted off, and their countenance was instantly changed. It looked radiant, glowing, and joyous; all the burden was gone, and a peace remained.

This is what deliverance can accomplish and why prayer is vitally important. My personal angel, Phillip, instructed me to press on and press in.

Understanding of Sin

Another morning, Jesus greeted me. He brought me to come and sit at the Lord's table. In the distance, I could see a church that I frequented in the spirit. The Father sat beside me and spoke, "My beloved son, you are so loved." As He spoke, I was reflecting on a disturbing dream I had had the night before. He continued, "Do you see the damage that sin causes? Just a little can influence you and your gifting in many ways. This dream was a way that one of your prophetic expressions was affected by being in contact with sin, flesh, and soul. This is why living from the spirit is vital to living and seeing rightly." He continued with the verse from Galatians 5:9 about a little leaven working its way through the whole batch. He said,

Although a harmless thing may not seem to have a large impact, its impact can be vast. This dream you are thinking of was not of Me or from Me, but as a matter of choice, I allowed an opportunity to see the effects of such things on My children. See yourself from Heaven's perspective; indulge yourself in Me.

Father said,

This battle has been won on the cross; surrender to Me fully, walking spirit first and in true sonship.

As I reengaged Heaven later that evening, the Father continued our dialogue from earlier that day. He said:

My son, be faithful in the small things, and you will see the double doors of favor open up.

Holy Spirit comforted me with His words and said,

The Lord's blessings are on your life, and you're stepping into a new season of glory-carrying, soul-winning, revelation-receiving, and miracles unlike that which you have ever seen. Stay yielded to the spirit, press into the Father's heart, press into new revelation, and seek greater intimacy because all you have experienced and seen is about to be intensified a thousandfold!

Chapter 21
Pressing Through Opposition

As I was being ministered to one day, Jesus said to me,

> *My son, press through the second heaven, there is much chaos and witchcraft in that atmosphere. As we near the vernal equinox, those upon the earth lost in darkness and hopelessness are at work doing their wicked deeds. However, the sons of righteousness have access to press through this thickened veil, to draw out the refreshing of the third heaven.*
>
> *Draw upon the living waters; the rainbow rivers of crystal clarity will refresh your weary soul and tired body. Allow Wisdom's life-giving essence to enfold you into her arms and allow her to guide you on all your paths. Never believe that you are less than worthy of My affections and deepest love, for your sin's debts were paid when I was laid upon the cross. All eternity cries out for justice to be delivered onto the earth. I know this moment in your history seems*

chaotic and burdensome, but it's for such a time as this and a season as this you were called for.

As Jesus was talking, a woman in white appeared; It was Esther. She spoke to me and said, "Child, do you know who I am?" I nodded yes. She said that wickedness will never triumph over the God of all creation. In every age, the power of hell has tirelessly tried to do what they do (kill, steal, and destroy). Time and time again, they are beaten back by the sons of God of the age and the war of Heaven's armies. Defeated foes will always remain defeated foes. I challenge you, son of God, to laugh in the face of adversity!

A Message for the Daughters of the King

At another point in time, I heard Heaven say,

'Be still and know the Lord will fight for you; this is the dawning of a new day. For I know the plans I have for you,' said the Lord God, 'plans for good and not for evil, plans to prosper you and not for calamity, plans to expand you and to redeem you, to give you a future and a hope.'

Today, I bestow upon you the tools of expanded faith to persist through the pressing and to conquer through the crushing, to know the perfect work of the Lord is being accomplished in you.

My son, I want you to look at every one of My daughters you meet as a sister or a mother. To them, you will look like a prince. I want you to emulate Jesus and tell them of the beauty I see in them.

Put behind you the ways the world has tainted your mind with an image of what a female should look like or what 'attractive' is. To me, that image is putrid and rotten. It is skin deep, ridden with ugliness and insecurity, vanity, and compromise. However, the beauty I see lies in the heart and beyond that, in the soul and spirit. It is the beauty no eye can judge, for it can only be seen with the heart. Prophesy My love, adoration, affection, and enthrallment with who they are and who they belong to.

Many have lost sight of their identity because the identity of the world is corrupt; it is a farce. It tells them they are only good enough if their features are prominent and voluptuous, if their waists and thighs are skinny. I tell you this day, in My Kingdom, the features that matter to man matter not to God, but that which man condemns I lift and exalt. I celebrate the beauty that can only be found within: the pearls of compassion and grace, the fruit of the Holy Spirit that swells within the hearts of those the world puts aside.

Rest & Refreshing

As I was journaling at another time, Heaven told me,

You have a book in you, My child; its pages are still being written, but when it's time, it will come out. Let yourself be restored with spiritual tune-ups and refreshing when you are weary or your thoughts feel scattered. As you know, rest or Shabbat is a warfare tactic, but it's also a vital resource for success in business and ministry. When you are weary, remember to 'turn in here' (the Father's arms); in My soft embrace, you will find the flow of refreshment and empowerment.

The answer to all life's struggles is found in rest. Your mind will be re-equipped to deal with the things that dominate your thought life, which is trying to figure things out from the soul. The heart will be refreshed, running with fresh streams of love and compassion, and your body will be refreshed and overwhelmed with the presence of love. Remember when the battles draw long, and you are awake till the dawn, turn in here.

Rest is the quieting of your mind and soul realm from all busyness. It is the positioning of submission in intimacy and the path of least resistance to accomplish all you are called to do. Rest is the place where creativity can expand, completely unhindered. It is the place of limitless productivity, positioning, posture, and a destination for the saints to be poised from.

Envision yourself as a child sitting upon the Father's lap on His throne. Sit back, relax, and administrate from this positioning. As you are encapsulated in His eternal love and rest, you will experience the confidence to do all things. You will find the deepest refreshing in this place, enabling you to press and persevere through the instances that ordinarily would seem untenable in the natural.

Overcoming Opposition

July 25th, 2022, I heard in the spirit, "Do you want to see the sick healed, the lame walk, and the blind see? Then, walk in unity with me, putting away the old mindsets. Put away the thought forms that are lies of this world and seek first the Kingdom of God. Father judges the hearts of those He so loves. The lawless He does not bring correction to; the scoffers and mockers get their teeth broken but do not have/know the need for repentance. Rend your heart and not your garments; hail the king of Heaven and Earth. Humble yourself in His sight; He will make you a great nation. Abandon pride and rejoice in distress, and He will lift you up.

Do not allow your soul to feel hollow and mislead you into neglecting spiritual truth. Walk with me, and I will give you rest."

As I heard this, I saw Jesus extend His hand to me. I was stuck in mud, and He lifted and pulled me out of it. He cleaned me off; instantly, I was transformed, wearing a white tuxedo glowing in the radiant light of His Glory. He asked me to dance with Him, and I wept.

He said, "Little one, do not worry; you have done marvelously in this season. It may not feel like a triumph, but you have conquered and overcome. Focus on what you have done right."

In Heaven, I could hear singing. I saw many saints, children, and angels worshipping Him. They sang, "We have overcome by the blood of the lamb and the words of our testimony."

Two birds flew in with a white sash with blue letters that said the word "Overcomer." He put it on me with a new crown and gave me a bouquet of white roses with baby breath.

Jesus said, "Overcoming looks like enduring in trials and persisting in distress."

I could see the Father saying, "Well done." I also saw the Lion of Judah, and I said, "Hail, hail, Lion of Judah." I could hear a chant in Heaven,

Hail, hail, Lion of Judah, let the lion roar.

As the Lion of Judah roared, I could see darkness being chased away by the frequency of the sound of the roar of the Lion. I said, "Roar over my life, my children, my marriage, my spouse, the desert places and the wilderness places."

As he roared, I saw darkness flee from each of these territories. I could see angels weeping as this deliverance from darkness took place.

I said, "Roar over my home, this county, our town, and church." As I spoke this, I saw the Lion lunge and sink its teeth into the throat of the spirit of religion and rip it out.

I heard Father speak in a commanding voice, "No longer will the spirit of religion plague and oppress you and your house and your tribe, for you have been tested, and you have been found to be mine!"

I just started worshipping the Father; I heard the words, "You have done valiantly, son of God."

"Endure in distress, persist in prayer, you will OVERCOME!"

Rejoicing in hope, enduring in distress, persisting in prayer. (Romans 12:12) (TLV)

Raising Up Others

When I stepped into Heaven on November 10th, 2021, I saw an elevator. It was all gold; the side walls were mirrors that reflected our image as the Father sees us. There was a red royal carpet inside and a glass back wall that overlooked all the earth. I pushed the button H3 for 3rd Heaven. As the elevator rose, I saw first all the earth, then all the second Heaven, planets, stars, and galaxies, and finally, it stopped. As the doors opened, I could see the glorious golden light of Heaven, with Jesus and my angels, Phillip and Lilly, at my sides.

We stepped out into a place called the Hall of Mandates. It was filled with many scrolls of mandates, some sealed for later times and some unsealed for such a time as this. I could see angels appearing, grabbing scrolls, and disappearing to bring them into the earth to those carrying out these Heavenly mandates.

I noticed an enormous angel guarding a big door marked, "For the Last Day." I got the impression that whatever is behind that door correlates with the end of the book of Revelation and that it would be released into the earth in its appointed time and season.

I noticed a golden scroll in the center of the room calling to my spirit as I approached it. I could hear it saying, "Rise up, raise up." My angel Phillip said, "This is your mandate at this moment, to rise as a leader, an ambassador of Heaven, to raise others in discipleship and the wisdom of heavenly realities."

Prophetic Burdens

On May 31st, 2022, the Lord spoke to me. He said, "What you have experienced, child, is a physical manifestation of what has run rampant through My Bride and churches. It has rendered them powerless; you are going through the Refiner's fire now, for where you step next, you cannot take this with you. This is being done in My love for you; you are so connected and yoked to Me that you have given yourself wholly and unreservedly to Me. The pull of sin and separation from My presence you have experienced has been a demonstration prophetically; My prophets often have felt the physical burden of My heart for My people; this is the burden you are feeling. Do not wallow in it; don't let it sap you; turn into me. Intercede for My people, for what you are experiencing is only a momentary weakness compared to the lifetimes of misery that My servants have been ensnared by. They have been dragged away to death by forsaking My covenant and My promises, choosing the evil Satan has unleashed in their minds, hearts, and churches."

To the angel of Messiah's community in Thyatira, write: 'Thus says the Son of God, who has eyes like a flame of fire and feet like polished bronze: I know your deeds and your love and faith and service and patient endurance, and that your last deeds are greater than the first. But this I have against you, that you tolerate that woman Jezebel, who calls herself a prophetess—yet she is teaching and deceiving My servants to commit sexual immorality and to eat food sacrificed to idols. I gave her time to repent, but she refuses to repent of her immorality. Behold, I will throw her into a sickbed, and those who commit adultery with her into great tribulation—unless they repent of her doings. I will also strike her children with a deadly disease. Then all of Messiah's communities will know that I am the One who searches minds and hearts, and I will give to each of you according to your deeds. But to the rest of you in Thyatira, who do not hold to this teaching and have not learned the so-called 'deep things' of Satan—I place on you no other burden. Only hold firm to what you have until I come. To the one who overcomes and guards My deeds until the end, 'I will give him authority over the nations, and he shall rule them with an iron rod, as when clay pots are broken into pieces.' Even as I have received from My Father, so I will give him the morning star. He who has an ear, let him hear what the Ruach is saying to Messiah's communities.' (The Revelation 2:18-29) (TLV)

Characters in this Book

Daphne: An angel assigned to assist me in the realms of Heaven.

Gloria: A woman in white linen, part of my cloud of witnesses, who assists me with writing.

Stewart: A man in white linen, part of my cloud of witnesses.

Dana: A man in white linen, part of my cloud of witnesses.

Enoch: An Old Testament patriarch.

Matthew: A New Testament patriarch.

Gabriel: A messenger angel.

Uriel: An angel who brought me a scroll from Heaven.

Robert: A man in white who assisted me in an engagement.

William: A man in white who assisted me in an engagement.

Malcom: A man in white who brings instruction from Heaven.

Mandy: A woman in white who is the advisor for the entity of Heaven Down Business.

Frequency: Chief angel over Heaven Down Business.

Mack: Angel assigned to Heaven Down Business.

Breakthrough: Angel assigned to Heaven Down Business.

Francisco/Frank: A man in white who assisted me in an engagement.

Mitchell: A man in white who brings instruction from Heaven.

Jeremiah: An Old Testament prophet.

Moses: An Old Testament patriarch.

Abraham: An Old Testament patriarch.

King David: An Old Testament monarch.

Phillip: My Chief personal angel.

Gregory: A man in white who instructed me in an engagement.

Francisco/Frank: A man in white who assisted me in an engagement in Heaven's Health Center.

Faith: An entity that instructed me in an engagement.

Samuel: An Old testament prophet.

Isaiah: An Old testament prophet.

Description

The Ancient Pathways of Heaven is more than a book; it's an invitation to heavenly exploration by faith.

For those who know that Holy Spirit dwells within them; for those who know the Father and are covenanted to Jesus and willing to enter the heavenly realms through Him as the gate... *The Ancient Pathways of Heaven* beckons explorers of faith.

This captivating book takes us on a spiritual journey with Jeremy Friedman as he explores the heavenly realms by faith. Each chapter recounts Jeremy's personal encounters, painting vivid pictures of Jesus, men and women in white, and other heavenly beings. These encounters bring deep revelation as he discovers ancient doors and paths, gates, dimensions, star gates, Destiny Scrolls, the commissioning of angels, quantum shifts, and more, providing readers with rich insights for contemplation. Each revelation gives the reader something to consider. *The Ancient Pathways of Heaven* will inspire and encourage you to enter the heavens and access the ancient pathways yourself.

About the Author

Jeremy Friedman is a prophetic teacher, evangelist, intercessor, and entrepreneur with an apostolic grace. He has an amazing testimony of how God saved his life and through his journey in finding the Lord he has helped many others learn the heart of the Father. His prophetic gifting allows him to see the world in a unique way that often can be missed by the naked eye. Jeremy seeks the Lord daily with his whole heart to learn and receive revelation from Heaven to help build God's Kingdom here on earth. As a Jewish believer in Yeshua, his heart is to be a bridge to all nations, to help them know that they are grafted into the rich Jewish Heritage of the Bible through our Messiah.

Currently he is the founder of Lighthouse Family Ministries, host of the Frequency of Heaven podcast, head coach for Heaven Down Business™, and a part of the LifeSpring International Ministries team. Jeremy has a desire to show others the pathways to freedom that he himself has been brought through in deliverance ministry. He is a devoted husband and father to five beautiful children who truly desires to see them walk in their callings and teach their generations to rise and build the Kingdom of Heaven.

www.ingramcontent.com/pod-product-compliance
Lightning Source LLC
Chambersburg PA
CBHW031629160426
43196CB00006B/345